THE Well-Adjusted Child

THE Well-Adjusted Child

HOW TO NURTURE THE EMOTIONAL HEALTH OF YOUR CHILDREN

Dr. Phil E. Quinn

Thanks for caring!

Yurian
Zhang

From one to Another —
I'm glad you
survived.

THOMAS NELSON PUBLISHERS
Nashville • Camden • New York

Publishers since 1798

Published in Nashville, Tennessee, by Thomas Nelson,
Inc., and distributed in Canada by Lawson Falle, Ltd.,
Cambridge, Ontario.

Printed in the United States of America.

To avoid grammatical problems, the pronouns *he* and
his have been used predominantly and do not reflect
sexism on the part of the publisher or author.

Library of Congress Cataloging-in-publication Data

Quinn, P. E. (Phil E.), 1950-
  The well-adjusted child.

  Bibliography: p. 151
  1. Parenting. 2. Child psychology. I. Title.
HQ755.8.Q56   1986   649'.1   86-23720
ISBN 0-8407-3061-6 (pbk.)

10 9 8 7 6 5 4

*To my daughter
Dixie Morgan
and all children, everywhere, with the
hope that they may all be blessed with
healthy childhoods*

The Well-Adjusted Child

Contents

Acknowledgments

Completing a project such as this always involves more people than the one name appearing on the front cover. Many of the technical people who worked on this book are unknown even to me. But they know who they are and the role they played in making it possible. To them and to my editor, Larry Weeden, I offer my sincere thanks and deepest appreciation for a job well done.

To all the brave people who allowed me brief glimpses into their lives as a way to demonstrate a point, I am particularly indebted. Without their willingness to help, my task would have been much more difficult. It was often their courage that fueled my own during times of greatest despair.

Always there are special people behind a work such as this whose gifts are less tangible than others', perhaps, but of unimaginable value nonetheless. I was blessed with two such special people, Fairy Caroland and Sandy Binkley. I cannot measure the value of their belief in me and their support of my work. Their reading of the manuscript, their comments and suggestions, and their unwavering encouragement throughout propelled me onward, even at times when my every instinct was to resign in defeat.

To my wife, Melissa, I owe my greatest tribute. Always there, always patient, always understanding, she wove a world of infinite peace and comfort about me as I labored painfully through troubled thoughts and difficult ideas. Her wisdom and insights enhanced the quality of this book. Her caring broadened its meaning, while her faith empowered its purpose. It is as much a product of her heart as of my mind.

Introduction

Melissa was so excited! This was going to be the happiest day of her life. For weeks she had waited eagerly for her birthday to arrive, carefully marking off each passing day on the calendar in her room. How hard it had been not to remind her family as the day grew nearer. But true to the promise she had made her mother when they discussed the birthday party weeks before, Melissa had bitten her tongue and resisted the temptation. Not once had she mentioned the party since that day. That was the agreement. Her mother had promised the party, but only if Melissa didn't nag her about it.

Melissa really didn't mean to nag her mother. But with four other children in the family, her father, family pets, a job, neighbors and friends, church, and several volunteer committees constantly competing for her mother's time and energy, it was sometimes hard for Melissa to hold her mother's attention long enough to discuss something so important. She was the only one among her friends who had never had a birthday party.

Not wanting to disturb her busy mother by asking for money to purchase party invitations, Melissa laboriously made them by hand, each one different from the others. After all eight were finished, she placed them in separate envelopes, careful to address them correctly, and piled them neatly on the edge of the sewing machine where her mother would be sure to find them. Checking the next day, Melissa was overjoyed to find the invitations gone. She was sure they were in the mail on their way to invite her most favorite friends in all the world to share her special day.

Happily, that special day had finally arrived! At last it was going to be her turn to be the princess for a day—the birthday girl wearing the beautiful crown of sparkling rhinestones and colored glass her friends passed around to wear at their parties. It was her turn to be the center of attention, to receive the warm hugs, happy smiles, and brightly wrapped gifts from all the others. She had waited so long for this day!

Hardly able to contain her excitement, Melissa waltzed through the morning as though in a dream, her mind filled with the fantasies of a child wanting desperately to feel special.

After helping with the lunch dishes, Melissa locked herself in the bedroom to begin preparing herself for the party. It was to start at three o'clock. Giving meticulous attention to every detail of her grooming, she slowly and carefully transformed the image in the mirror from a plain, ordinary girl in an ordinary house on an ordinary day into a majestic princess radiating beauty, elegance, and grace on her way to a lavish ball being held in her honor in the palace ballroom. It was that special day each year when people from all over the kingdom came eagerly to celebrate the birthday of their beloved princess. With a final, critical glance in the mirror, the princess was at last ready to receive her court of admirers.

Hesitating at the bedroom door, Melissa decided to remain in her room until all the guests had arrived and the summons came from her mother. What an entrance she would make walking slowly down the stairs into the room filled with beautiful decorations and cheering friends!

Patiently, Melissa waited. Three o'clock came and went. There was no sound to be heard from downstairs. Three-fifteen. Then three-thirty. What was happening? Where was everybody? Why didn't her mother call her downstairs for the party? she wondered nervously as she stared blindly at the clock. Did something go wrong?

Fighting the panic that made her stomach hurt, Melissa could wait no longer. Maybe it was going to be a surprise party and everyone was quietly hiding, waiting for her to come down the stairs so they could jump out from everywhere as she entered. That was it, of course! A surprise party. *What a wonderful idea,* she thought as her confidence and excitement returned.

Bubbling with anticipation, her young, tender heart pounding in her throat, Melissa opened the bedroom door and stepped into the hallway. She was greeted with a silence full of promises.

It was a short walk to the stairs. Fully prepared for the big surprise, Melissa was not prepared for what she saw as the living room at the bottom of the stairs slowly came into view. It was empty! There were no lights, no decorations, no music, no presents piled high on the coffee table, no smiling, cheering friends. There was no party for her, none at all.

Her dreams shattered into a lifetime of fragments, a part of Melissa died along with her fantasy that ordinary afternoon. The magic in her special day was gone. Depressed and feeling sick in her stomach, she spent the rest of the afternoon crying out her pain in the pillow on her bed. In an agony that would mark the rest of her life, Melissa was overwhelmed by her simple unimportance. There was nothing special about her. Nothing at all.

It was hard having dinner with her family that evening, pretending to be pleased as they celebrated her birthday in the usual manner after the meal. They were surprised when she declined the cake and ice cream and excused herself early to go to bed. Although she appreciated their efforts, it just wasn't the same.

While cleaning house several days later, Melissa found the small stack of handmade party invitations in a cabinet drawer. They were still in their envelopes, just as she had left them. They never had been mailed.

Dreams and Realities

It would be difficult for the child in us not to empathize with Melissa. When she first described this event from her childhood to me, I could feel her pain and disappointment. I hurt for her then as you must hurt for her now. We were all children once and can remember our own desperate need to feel special. If we take a moment and empty our thoughts of adult concerns, we can also remember how important our hopes and dreams were in fashioning our childhoods.

Childhood dreams serve a dual purpose. On the one hand, they provide much of the hope that inspires us to learn and grow. Through our dreams we can take what is and make it into what could be; we can look beyond the ordinary to see the miracle of which we are a part. It is through our dreams that we can best see the possibilities that exist within our limits, the "mights" and "maybes" that inspire us to be more than we are. What would we be without our dreams?

Just as important, childhood dreams serve to protect the vulnerable hearts and minds of our children from the harsh and often painful realities of a world over which they have no control. They make reality bearable. Their dreams can make them the center of attention even in a crowd too busy to notice, or make them feel loved and wanted in a world too preoccupied with its own concerns to care. Dreams help them feel special even when those they love the most seem to tell them different.

So as I listened to Melissa's story for the first time, one part of me empathized with her. Another part of me, however, had quite a different reaction. Perhaps you did, too. The adult in me had a hard time taking her problem seriously. Missing a birthday party hardly seems important when compared to the concerns you and I face every day as adults. What are the hurt feelings of a child compared to our struggle to keep her fed and in clothes and shoes? Or the daily grind we must suffer through to earn a living? To pay the rent and car note? Or the pressure we feel to raise our children properly and protect them from drugs, molesters, and exploiters who would do them harm? How important are hurt feelings when compared to the endless sacrifices we make for our children?

From such a worldly perspective, it would be difficult for me as a parent to take Melissa's hurt feelings seriously. After all, there would be other birthdays. Melissa is not the only child to be deprived of a party on her tenth birthday. She would get over it soon enough. No real harm done.

Yet, even as the adult in me brings reassurance that no permanent damage has been done to Melissa, the child in me sharing her hurt is not so sure. If no real harm was done, why would she remember it with such pain so many years later as an adult? As a child growing up in her family, Melissa celebrated many birthdays before she left home. Why is it that the only one that stands out clearly in her memory is the tenth birthday? Clearly, some childhood experiences mean more to us than others and so are remembered, while others are not. Some childhood experiences help us, while others hurt us. Some build us up, while others tear us down. Some inspire us, while others fill us with despair.

All parents make mistakes that sometimes hurt their children. But hurting a child and damaging a child are different. Hurts can heal. Scars never can.

Just what dynamics were at work in this situation? What was going on? And more important, how did Melissa interpret what was happening?

The first thing we can see is that there was a betrayal of trust. Melissa and her mother had an agreement. The mother would provide a party as long as Melissa didn't nag her about it. The child kept her end of the agreement, but the mother didn't keep hers.

Something important happens in a relationship when promises are broken. Betrayal of basic trust in the relationship between parent and child can mentally and emotionally damage the child—perhaps even cripple her for life. To develop normally, children must be able to trust their parents. Their trust is destroyed when hopes and dreams entrusted to their parents are shattered through carelessness or when their basic needs are ignored by the only people capable of meeting them. Or when promises are not kept.

Second, Melissa's mother unknowingly conveyed to her the message that she and her birthday were unimportant and not worthy of the mother's time and effort. Children learn early that people remember and act upon those opportunities and obligations they consider to be most important. Significant events get a lot of attention; whereas unimportant matters receive little or no consideration.

You can imagine how Melissa interpreted what happened to her. Although there are many possible reasons why her parents chose not to give her the party, Melissa won't know the real reason unless they tell her. She came to believe that she knew the reason: she was unworthy of it and didn't deserve the effort involved.

Third, the failure of Melissa's mom to provide a party was part of a pattern of accumulated disappointments in the young girl's life. I mentioned at the beginning of Melissa's story that she had constant and heavy competition for her mother's attention. The party that never happened was not the first time Melissa had been made to feel unimportant. If it had been, her hurt wouldn't have been so severe. Usually no single event, however traumatic, will emotionally scar a child for life. Because this disappointment capped a succession of similar experiences, however, it was especially devastating—much like the proverbial straw that broke the camel's back.

While we usually notice the major problems and big crisis events in our children's lives, it's easy to overlook the little things that hurt them, the small disappointments and broken promises that are remembered over the years and can have a devastating, cumulative effect on their lives. As parents, we may forget the individual hurts, but our children won't if that becomes the pattern of their lives.

While major crises can damage, most often it is the cumulative effect of many little hurts over a long time that hinders a child's growth and development.

Fourth, Melissa's mother forgot a principle that all parents lose sight of from time to time: what may be unimportant to an adult may be extremely important to a child. Likewise, a parent cannot measure the effect of an event on a child by its effect on her as an adult. In other words, to appreciate how events affect our children, we need to work at seeing those happenings from their perspective, not ours.

What may be unimportant to an adult may be vitally important to a child. It is often a mistake to measure the effect of an event on a child by how it affects an adult.

It's easy for parents to make this mistake. From the very beginning, all of us have to make decisions concerning what's important and what isn't important in the lives of our children. Most often these decisions are based on what's especially important to *us*. The more preoccupied we become with adult matters, the more likely we are to dismiss the affairs of our children as unimportant. Naturally, our perception of the problem will determine how we respond to it—or whether we respond at all. Problems we consider insignificant will not be taken as seriously or result in the same amount of attention and effort on our part as will those we perceive as serious threats to the welfare of our children.

Effects and Reactions

The emotional harm Melissa suffered stayed with her into adulthood, which points to the simple fact that adult personalities are largely shaped by childhood experiences. Some emotionally traumatic events in childhood are never forgotten or outgrown. They become a permanent part of us, a source of perpetual pain that may well determine the pace and posture of our walk through life. A physically disfigured child, for example, may be so emotionally wounded by the ongoing teasing and ridicule of other children that he spends the rest of his life avoiding contact with people. It is also possible for a physically healthy child to be emotionally handicapped. Indeed, a twisted self-image is no less a handicap than a twisted leg. Both will inhibit the child's functioning, and emotionally troubled children rarely grow into healthy, well-adjusted adults.

There's one more truth you need to know about at this point, however—it will be developed in depth in the following chapters—and it's our source of hope. What you've read so far may have discouraged you as you realize that all parents occasionally make mistakes like that of Melissa's mother. But what you also need to understand is that the negative event itself, such as Melissa's being deprived of a birthday party, is not as important to the child's long-term emotional health as *how the parents respond* to what happens. And here is where wisdom and love can overcome our unintended parental mistakes.

Not long ago, my young son came running into the house from the back yard holding the index finger of his right hand. I saw fear, pain, and questioning in his eyes as he showed me the finger. It was bleeding from a small scratch. Taking him into the bathroom, I washed the wound, sprayed it with disinfectant, and wrapped the finger snugly in a bandage. After a warm smile and some reassurance from me that he was going to be all right, my son returned to play in the back yard. By evening the bandage was gone, the scratch and the event that caused it long forgotten.

Had I reacted with panic and alarm at the sight of blood oozing from his finger, however, the emotional outcome for him could have been quite different. Because children tend to interpret the importance and seriousness of events in their lives by watching parental reactions, I could easily have taken the minor hurt of a scratch on the finger and made it into a major crisis in which the poor child might have feared for his life.

On the other hand, if I had ignored my son, scolded him for making so much fuss over such a minor injury, or laughed at his childish concern, I would have conveyed to him that I didn't care, that his hurts are not important, and that bringing his hurts to me will only result in my adding even more hurt to them. Clearly, this also would have been an inappropriate response.

One of the greatest challenges for all parents is to learn appropriate reactions to their children in constantly changing situations. It is important to the emotional health of children that parents avoid both extremes of underreaction and overreaction. Denying a problem where one exists and creating a problem where one did not exist are equally inappropriate responses that can harm children.

Notice, however, that if we're sensitive to our children and can be aware of when they're hurting, the importance of our response gives us an opportunity to bring healing to our children and the restoration of their confidence in our love and willingness to meet their needs. We can offer them the reassurance that whatever their hurt, it will pass and life will go on. If we're the cause of the hurt, we can apologize and help them understand that while we make mistakes from time to time, our love for and commitment to them never waver.

Parenting as a Ministry

An invitation by God for us to share in His procreative process by bearing children is also a call to the ministry of parenthood. Just as Mary and Joseph were called by God to be parents for our Lord Himself, so are all parents called by the Creator to minister to those among us most precious in His sight—children.

Children and childhoods are dear to God. If they are preserved, out of them will flow God's purpose. Yet one cannot thrive without the other. Together children and childhoods must be nurtured and protected.

The right to have children also involves a responsibility to raise them, to be good stewards of the young lives entrusted into our care. It involves a desire to be the best parents possible and a commitment to the Father of us all to raise one of His own as one of us.

The difference between successful parents who flourish in their ministry and those who flounder unsuccessfully cannot be found in their intentions. Most parents want and strive for what they believe is best for their children. Their intentions are good, they mean well, and they want to be faithful to their calling. The difference between successful and unsuccessful parents is in the *effectiveness* of their love and caring, which requires knowledge and skills such as we'll discuss in this book.

God does not call us into the ministry of parenthood to fail. Rather, His intention is that we succeed. Remember that as you read this book and strive each day to be a better parent, which this book is designed to help you do. I want you to become more aware, better prepared, and more capable of meeting the emotional needs of your child while avoiding the pitfalls that would do him harm. My purpose is not to make you feel guilty about your mistakes or to make you feel you are failing as a parent. What I hope to do is take the love and caring you have for your child and direct it into more effective parenting. What is needed from you is an open mind and heart to receive a deeper understanding of children and childhood.

In Part 1, you will learn the difference between good and bad touches and between change that stimulates and change that overwhelms. You will learn about words that build up and words that destroy; about silence that brings peace and silence that causes pain. You will also learn how too much control and too much suffering in a family can actually inhibit a child's growth and development. Then in Part 2, you will learn how successful, thriving families differ from those that seem burdened with problems and are barely able to survive. All these elements can help you care more effectively for your child. And perhaps by learning to identify some of the pitfalls along the way, you will be able to avoid them as you raise your child. For every fall we prevent, we add just that much more strength to the generation that will soon replace us as keepers of the kingdom.

Through effective caring, parents can transform ordinary childhoods into magical moments of limitless possibility, the parenting task into an exciting adventure of growth and change, and the inevitable hurts along the way into a more profound sense of love, health, and hopefulness. Together, parent and child can experience the joys and rewards of God's purpose fulfilled in their relationship and watch in wonder and awe as the mystery of the Creator's image becomes His reflection in the glow of a child's face.

Part 1
The Unintentional Harm We Can Do

Chapter 1
Where Are You Taking My Bed?

Recently, I had to watch my adolescent daughter hug her best friend good-bye. Her family was moving to another state far away. It warmed my heart to see them care so deeply about each other, yet I was saddened because of the emptiness that would follow.

As I watched them struggle painfully with the farewell, I was reminded that it had not always been this way between these two. I remembered the early days of their relationship. Those were days spent trying to avoid each other, daring not to speak or smile, pretending not to notice the other's presence. It was like a cat-and-mouse game they would play to attract the other's attention without appearing interested. How hard they tried not to be friends!

Then came the day of discovery. It was a miracle that surprised them both. They had given so much attention to not giving the other any attention that they inadvertently discovered something about the other they liked! They found themselves wanting to spend time together, to get to know each other better.

Pursuing their curiosity, they soon found other things to like about each other—as well as things to dislike. Oh, how tempers flared from time to time! And what hurt feelings! Despite their vows never to speak again, they always did. Their friendship continued to grow. Sooner or later one or the other would break the ice with a smile or a phone call, and off they would go again in the relationship.

I marveled at the complexity and beauty of their evolving relationship. It was like a flower slowly opening itself to full blossom. Tentative and frightened at first, they had gone through five years of unfolding to arrive at this point of deepest caring. Now, suddenly, they were having to say good-bye.

Their relationship was undergoing a radical change over which they had no control. Like all change, it was bringing them both joy and pain. Joy for the love they shared and the place they had in each other's life. Pain because the relationship would never again be the same. Better perhaps. More important maybe. But no longer the same. It would be different, and they would have to get used to that difference. And as the relationship changed, they would change. Time would change. The world around them would change. Everything would change.

Watching the two of them reminded me there is nothing more certain in life than change. It is everywhere, within us and around us. From one moment to the next, day after day, everything changes. Nothing remains the same. Life is a constantly unfolding revelation. Each day brings new knowledge, new understanding, and a deeper meaning to life in this time and place. Our attitudes, beliefs, values, hopes, and dreams change as we mature and grow in wisdom. We change our appearance, our clothing, and our behavior as life offers more opportunities for experiencing its possibilities. Occasionally, we change houses, jobs, schools, and churches. In the process we make new friends as we leave old friends behind. Everything changes.

Understanding the Effects of Change

Some change is good. Slow, gradual change over a long period of time can help us grow and mature. It can help us function better in our relationships, at school, and on the job. Getting an education is a change that is going on constantly over many years and results in great benefits.

Some change is not good. It, too, occurs over a long period of time. It can occur so gradually that we do not recognize it until it becomes a serious problem threatening our health or welfare. Bad change tends to interfere with our everyday functioning. Ulcers and heart disease, for example, tend to evolve over a period of time. Other change can be sudden and dramatic, as when a family member dies unexpectedly or we get an unexpected promotion.

Some change is unavoidable. Eliminating all change from our lives is impossible. Some of it is forced upon us by people and life situations over which we have no control. How many of us would like to stay young for a while longer than we do? But there is no stopping the aging process once it has begun.

Some change is self-initiated. We bring about the changes ourselves, as when we decide to do something differently, break a habit, or change our mind about something.

Regardless of what kind or its source, all change causes physical and emotional stress. Stress results from our attempt to keep internal conditions stable and constant despite changing conditions around us. Stress is what we feel, for example, as we try to stay calm in the middle of a crisis or an embarrassing situation. It is the discomfort of stress that motivates us to do what must be done to relieve it, to become comfortable again.

Too much stress caused by excessive change can result in physical or emotional *dis*tress. As we struggle to cope and adapt to change in our lives, we may become angry or depressed or we may experience panic and feel desperately out of control. We may become physically sick or do and say things out of character for us. We may make foolish decisions we later regret. We may even become so overwhelmed that we give up, surrendering our wills to chance, and withdraw into a sense of personal failure.

Some changes consistently cause more distress than others. A serious illness causes someone more stress than watching his child strike out with the bases loaded. The changes causing the greatest concern are those that threaten what we consider most important and value most highly—our homes, family, health, career.

On the positive side, as well as adding spice to life, some change keeps life interesting. It provides us stimulation and opportunities to learn and grow. It exposes us to new situations and different people, and it helps us develop our coping skills. *In most cases, it is the extremes of not enough change and too much change that cause the most problems.*

Children can be emotionally damaged by too much change too quickly. It can overwhelm their ability to cope.

Children are particularly vulnerable to change. They have so little control over what happens to them. For those of us who have ever experienced it, we know how frightening it can be to lose all control of a situation—particularly when there is a threat of harm to us. Such feelings of total vulnerability can have a serious emotional impact on us. The same is true for children, but more so.

Too much change can overwhelm a child's infantile ability to adjust, to cope and understand. In time, the pressure may prove too great for his developing emotional defenses, and serious harm may result when those defenses collapse. Such was my own case as a child moved from one foster home to another, and then another and another, many times during the early years of my life. After a while I could no longer cope with all the changes, the people coming in and moving out of my life so quickly, the houses, rooms, yards, and schools that kept changing. I gave up and quit trying to adjust at all. I decided people could not be trusted to be there for me, so I withdrew into myself—a private little world unaffected by all the turmoil around me. It was the only place I felt safe and secure.

Children can be emotionally damaged by not enough change over a long period of time. It can result in feelings of boredom, apathy, and hopelessness.

On the other hand, life without stimulation, meaning, purpose, and challenge is boring. Energy and interest levels may drop, the child may become dispirited and depressed. His sense of personal worth may be affected.

What parents of school-aged children have not witnessed the effects of the "summertime blues" on their kids? The problem usually begins the second or third week of summer vacation. After the initial excitement of being free of the rigorous demands of school has worn off, then begins the disturbing chorus of "I'm bored!" so familiar to parents. Within days this chorus is changed into a deep, wailing lament of "There's nothing to do!"

There is an optimum level of change in the lives of healthy children: enough to challenge and stimulate without overwhelming and destroying them.

A healthy balance of change will enhance rather than diminish a child's energy and interest level, his ability to learn, cope, and love. It will strengthen his emotional stability and increase his capacity for hope

Too Much Change

Our daughter was more than a year old when she finally slept most of the night. It took that long to get her into a sleep routine comfortable for all of us. What a joy it was for us to sleep more than a couple of hours at a time!

Then we decided to take her on an overnight trip to visit relatives in Atlanta. The child was wonderful on the trip down. And what a reception she received when we arrived! She even handled being passed endlessly from one pair of hands to another. But guess what happened when bedtime rolled around? The child went crazy. She started crying and wouldn't stop unless her mother was holding her. Several times she dozed off in her mother's arms, but she would wake up crying again when we tried to lay her in the bed. It was well past midnight before she finally went to sleep out of pure exhaustion. But even then she didn't sleep for more than an hour or two at a time. Even after returning home to her own bed and familiar surroundings, she still had trouble going to bed at night and staying asleep. It took us several months to get her back into a comfortable sleep routine.

What happened? Why did my child regress to an earlier stage of development?

What happened was too much change too quickly. After barely a year of getting acquainted with the people, objects, and places in the world around her, everything changed almost in an instant. Sights, sounds, smells, environmental conditions, even the people trying to hold her—everything changed. She had just gotten to the point where she felt reasonably safe and secure in the world around her. The fledgling trust she felt toward her parents to take care of her and meet her every need was seriously challenged for the first time.

Instead of stimulating and exciting the child as such a trip might an adult, all the sudden changes overwhelmed her infantile senses and capacity to understand and adapt. The result was enough emotional distress to disrupt her routines. Her behavior clearly communicated her distress.

Just as it is possible to disrupt routines with too much change, so it is possible to distort patterns of thought and behavior seriously enough to interfere with normal development. Too much change for too long can result in serious problems for the growing child. Consider the case of Mary.

Mary's father was a traveling salesman. Easily disillusioned, he moved from job to job looking for that one golden opportunity, that one chance in a lifetime that would turn his dreams into treasure. He was a hard worker and a dedicated family man. He wanted to provide his family the very best possible of all things. In an effort to do so, he pushed himself constantly, never satisfied with what he had, always with an eye open for a better opportunity somewhere else.

The result for Mary was tragic. I first met her at the age of twenty when she came to my office for counseling. She looked much older than her age and had that look of overwhelming fatigue and defeat in her eyes so familiar to those of us who work with desperate people. After hearing her story, I understood why and marveled that she was able to continue functioning at all.

By the time she was thirteen years old, Mary had lived in twelve different houses in twelve different cities and had attended classes in eight different schools. Because her family moved around so much, she was never able to make friends. Although she was attractive and intelligent, there were no special people in her life her own age. She was alone, except for her vast collection of stuffed animals.

Never in one place long enough, Mary wasn't able to develop any special skills or interests. She didn't participate in sports, play a musical instrument, cheerlead for a football team, enter a beauty contest, or go to dances, movies, or parties. She belonged to no youth clubs or organizations. She existed only as that good-looking girl everybody noticed but nobody knew.

Unable to deal effectively with the frequent school changes, Mary made poor grades. It wasn't that she couldn't do the work. She could. It was that other matters, more important at the time, took almost all her time and energy. Like trying to make a friend. Having to constantly compete with kids who had grown up together in the same neighborhood, Mary tried desperately to make a place for herself in groups of peers who would make no room for her. Frustrated and angry, she became more and more a behavioral problem at home and at school.

Finally, out of the desperation only a lonely, rejected adolescent can know, Mary turned to sex as a way to get the attention and acceptance she craved. It worked. She soon became one of the most popular girls at school—especially among the boys. The girls envied her popularity with the boys and sought her out as a companion.

Overwhelmed by her sudden popularity and the attention it brought, and riddled with guilt and shame by how she had earned it, Mary soon turned to drinking as a way to ease her emotional distress.

By fourteen she was pregnant. By sixteen she had experienced two abortions. By seventeen she was a high-school dropout and was married. By twenty she was single again and an alcoholic. This is when I met her for the first time.

Mary's case is an extreme example of what can happen to children who are forced to cope with too much change, too fast, and for too long. They are never given the opportunity to grow and develop normally.

Most of the pain and suffering in Mary's life could have been prevented had she received the emotional necessities of a healthy childhood. It wasn't that her parents didn't love and care about her. They did. A lot. Although they were aware of some of the difficulties the frequent moves and home changes caused Mary, they were sure she could cope with the circumstances and were totally unaware of the serious problems they would eventually cause their developing daughter until it was too late.

Mary's problems during adolescence and early adulthood were largely caused by childhood deprivations. Certain important needs were not met. And trying to meet childhood needs as an adult is not only futile, but also likely to result in serious problems. Desperate as an adolescent and a young adult, Mary attempted to meet her childhood need for intimacy and friendship using the lure of sex and then manipulating her partners into a relationship. None of the relationships provided her what she really wanted, and all of them brought her more grief and suffering.

What Mary needed most as a young child was what all children need early in life if they are to develop normally. She needed a home rather than a series of houses to live in. She needed a room that was her space to occupy, an intimate environment she could shape and fashion to reflect her unique personality. She needed teachers who had been around her enough to be able to get to know her as a person and be aware of her strengths and weaknesses, rather than as just another student in a class. She needed friends, people who cared about her and allowed her to care about them, people she grew up with sharing the inevitable highs and lows of life. She also needed a chance to discover her unique talents and abilities, and an opportunity to explore and develop them.

What Mary needed most was some consistency and permanence in her childhood. She needed for *some* things to remain the same and never change. She needed some of her relationships and certain parts of her environment to stay the same today, tomorrow, and the next.

Not all change in the lives of our children can be controlled. Nor should it be. But there are some areas in which too much change can be controlled. And in most cases, it should be. In those instances when dramatic change cannot be avoided, it is important that we parents at least minimize the emotional effects of it in the lives of our children.

Change Parents Can Control

The ability to trust is a cornerstone of emotional health. It is the foundation upon which much of the adult personality will be built. It shapes our thinking and beliefs about life, other people, and the world around us.

Developing a sense of trust is one of the first and most critical developmental tasks of early childhood. It is acquired through

11

early interaction with parents and the home environment. When children wake up day after day in the same room, with the same furniture and toys around them, the same sights, sounds, and smells today as yesterday and the day before, they feel secure in their environment. They learn there is nothing to fear about the world around them. As they come to know their environment, they soon begin mastering it and thereby gain a basic sense of trust that they are safe within it.

Likewise, when children see their parents are quick and eager to fulfill the basic needs they can't meet themselves, they learn they can trust and depend on their parents to take care of them. This makes children feel loved, wanted, and secure.

Trust is built over time through repetition. It can only evolve if there is consistency from one day to the next in the parent-child relationship. If there is continuity in the world around them, children learn the world is a predictable place over which they have a certain amount of control.

Trust cannot be built on change. The more things remain the same in early childhood, the greater the sense of trust and security our children develop. Life becomes orderly and manageable. Knowing what to expect from others and being able to count on predictable responses are the bases of trust. Doubt and uncertainty, on the other hand, breed anxiety and distrust, which tend to weaken relationships.

It is important that you build a sense of trust in your children by controlling certain changes in their lives, relationships, and environment.

Frequent Home and School Changes

Your children's world consists of two primary arenas of activity during the early, formative years. These are the home and the school (or the day-care center). Most of their waking hours will be spent in one of these two places.

After one of my recent parenting seminars, I received a letter from a mother concerned about the possible effects on her two-and-a-half-year-old son of a move to a new house. She wrote,

"My husband and I have been renting ever since we were married five years ago. Unable to find an apartment community we really liked, we moved around a lot (three times since Mark was born). At last we have a chance to buy a home. This is something we have both dreamed about for years! But I am concerned about Mark. He has friends where we now live and seems happy. After attending your seminar and hearing you talk about change, I am afraid of what another move might do to Mark. Should we forget the move for the sake of our son and just stay where we are? Or is there some way we can make the move easier for him?"

Ideally, children need to be exposed to as little change as possible during the early years of life. It is best for them if they are not moved too much from house to house, from one school to another, for the reasons stated earlier. In this case, however, the family was not moving to another temporary living situation, another apartment. The home they hoped to purchase represented what their son needed most—permanence and continuity. For that reason, I suggested they go ahead and make the move.

Sure, another move will affect Mark. But there are some things his parents can do to make the move less painful for him and thereby minimize any harm the move might do. Since this is such a common concern in our mobile society, let me list a few steps that will make a move to a new home easier for a child.

1 Begin preparing your child emotionally for the move by talking about it as far in advance of the move as possible. Abrupt surprises that catch us off guard and unprepared are often frightening and even overwhelming, especially for children.

2. Take your child to visit the new house as many times as possible before moving day. Show him where his room will be, where your room will be. Allow him to get acquainted with the house before you move in.

3. Spend some time allowing your child to imagine aloud what it will be like to live in the new house. Encourage him to

express his feelings about the move, both his anxieties and his excitement.

4. Before moving day, take as many of your child's personal things to the new house as possible. Allow *him* to carry them into the house and place them where *he* wants them in his room.

5. Once the furniture arrives, set up his room first, allowing him to help. Letting him participate in the move helps him feel he's part of what is happening to the family and not a victim of it.

6. *Do not* change the linens on your child's bed the first night in the new house. Instead, allow him to sleep amidst familiar smells the first couple of nights.

7. Be sure to follow usual bedtime routines. Do not allow the move to change family habits. Routines are important in helping children feel secure in the midst of change.

8. Spend some extra time with your child during the first few days in the new house. The more time and attention you can give him during the adjustment period, the easier it will be for him to make the necessary changes.

Being a good parent in the midst of a family move from one house to another means you take the time to care effectively. By doing the things I have suggested, the move can be an exciting adventure for the entire family.

A good rule of thumb when major change is essential is to *eliminate all unnecessary change.* Focus as much of your attention and your child's attention on the things that will remain the same as on those that will change. For a child, there is security in sameness and fear in change. Minimize the fear by maximizing your child's sense of security and trust. Your reward will be an easier transition from one house to another and the joy of an emotionally healthy child.

Domestic Chaos

One of the most difficult times of day for almost every family is dinner time. This is how one mother of three described it: "My husband and I both work. We take turns picking the kids up from the day-care center on our way home. By the time we get home, both of us are tired and want time alone. But it seems the more tired we are, the more the kids want from us! They swarm over me as I'm trying to prepare supper, tugging at my skirt and wrapping themselves around my legs. And the constant 'Mommy! Mommy!' It's all I can do sometimes to keep from screaming at them or hitting them to make them stop and leave me alone. Sometimes I get so mad I scare myself. I'm afraid some day I will lose control and really hurt one of them. It's all I can do some days just to get something—anything—on the table. And then there are baths, the dishes, the housework. It's crazy! I'm crazy!"

Sound familiar? It does to me! Even the most well-structured family will experience some domestic chaos from time to time, particularly during periods of crisis or great stress such as the family reunion after a long day apart, mealtimes, bath times, and bedtimes. Who among us has not experienced irritation and anger at children demanding our attention when we are desperately trying to finish important tasks?

But dinner time need not be chaotic in your family. It doesn't have to be a time you dread and wish you didn't have to experience every day. There are some things you can do to alleviate the stress, get dinner prepared and on the table, and make a traditional time of family disaster into one of the most prized times of family togetherness.

1. Somewhere between your work place and your first encounter with your kids at the front door of your home, do something to treat yourself. You have worked hard all day, probably without a word of thanks or appreciation. You deserve a treat. Anything will do: take a short walk through the park before heading home, stop for a soft drink, listen to your favorite music, or take a scenic route home. What is important is that you finish the work day and leave it behind before you try to interact with your kids. Clear your mind of what you have been doing all day, and focus it on the special time ahead with your family.

2. Upon entering the house, kick off your shoes, loosen the tie or belt, and usher your children as a group into the kitchen or

15

other family gathering place. Keep the family together even though what you want most is some time alone, a hot shower, or some aspirin for your headache.

3. Share a light snack with your children, something already prepared and just enough to satisfy their hunger temporarily without ruining their appetites for dinner.

4. While eating the snack, sit back, relax, and give your children your *undivided attention*. Children separated from their parents all day usually have many important things to tell them at the end of that day. Give them the attention they're craving. Let them show you their artwork, skinned knees, and whatever else is so important it can't wait. By giving them your undivided attention at the start of the evening, you will meet their attention needs and they will be less likely to hound you for attention throughout the evening.

5. Even though it may be difficult at times because you are tired and want to be doing something else, speak softly and directly to every child, calling each by name. Be physically and emotionally responsive to your children. Have you ever tried to impress someone who was not impressed or talk to a stone wall? It isn't very satisfying, is it? Be warm and affectionate with the children. Let them know you care—really care—about what has happened to them and what they have done during the day. Hold them in your lap, if possible. Or at least hug them. Nothing has more therapeutic value for a child than a hug.

6. After a half-hour or so, your children will likely be satisfied and want to pursue their own interests in the house or the back yard. Now is your time! Take a while to tend to your own need for comfort, attention, and relaxation. It's important that your needs are met, too. It's hard to give your children what you need yourself.

7. Develop and maintain comfortable routines for accomplishing tasks. A routine is a systematic approach to achieving a goal. Routines are important because they give purpose and direction to activity, make clear each family member's role and responsibilities, and result in successful accomplishment of the task with the least amount of time and effort.

16

8. Assign each of your children a task to perform to help with dinner. But a word of caution: be careful to spell out exactly what you expect from each child. Children want to meet parental expectations, but they cannot do so if they do not know what those expectations are. Do not make the mistake of assuming the children can figure it out for themselves. Be clear. Be specific.

9. Reward their efforts and cooperation with compliments. Praise each child's efforts and watch how much harder the child will work to please you. It's amazing what praise will do.

10. Resist the temptation to use this family time to discuss the unpleasant events of the day or family problems or to highlight the inadequacies of the children. *The focus of this time together should be on the positive and good things about life, the family, and one another.* This time should be used to make one another feel good. Set aside another special time for dealing with the bad stuff. Keep dinner-time conversation light, pleasant, and fun. Try to stimulate laughter. Do this and your entire family will be richly blessed.

Children, like adults, must have some order and structure in their lives. Although spontaneity is important and we must be careful not to overstructure the time we spend with them, our children need certain routines that are repeated each day. These routines help the family function smoothly and successfully, and kids can count on them to accomplish necessary tasks in times of crisis or upheaval in the family. Out of such routines evolve strong feelings of trust and security. They are the boundaries in which healthy children and families grow and flourish.

Family Crises

All families experience crises from time to time. Some are minor and easily managed, as in the case of misplaced car keys or burned supper. Others are more serious and challenge the continued existence of the family as a unit, as with the loss of a job or the death of a family member. But common to all crises is change.

Change is one of the primary sources of stress in our families. Change forces us to make adjustments we may not want to make, to alter the way we think or the way we do things. A serious problem in some families is the domino effect of change; that is, one change causes another, and that one causes yet another, and so on until the family finds itself caught in a threatening series of what appear to be unending changes.

Crises can also be emotionally damaging to children, who tend to look to their parents for guidance and support. Not knowing how to handle it, a child models his response to the crisis after that of his parents. If the parents panic, the child is likely to panic as well. *If adults cannot cope effectively with their problems, it is unrealistic to expect children to do so.*

The greatest fear of most children in a crisis is that when *some* things change, *all* things will change. For children, whose basic need is a sense of security, this can be emotionally overwhelming. Never are they confronted more brutally with their own helplessness than in the midst of crises they cannot stop or prevent. Such experiences can become damaging when their parents appear as helpless as themselves.

We cannot prevent all tragedies from occurring in the family. Nor can we eliminate all crises. But we can do two very important things. We can eliminate *unnecessary* crises from the lives of our children, and we can minimize the effect of unavoidable crises.

Avoiding unnecessary crises means that we do not allow ourselves to be petty. Many family crises are not really crises at all. They become crises because of our reactions. Most often, they're not nearly so important as to deserve the attention and effort we give them. For example, a child's spilling a glass of water is a common accident. It need not be a crisis in which there are angry words, spankings, hurt feelings, and great emotional distress.

You can help protect your child from crises by minimizing the possible harmful effects. Let me offer a few suggestions.

1. Make sure the issue at stake is important enough to result in a family crisis. Genuine crises usually are centered on threats

to the health, welfare, or functioning of the family as a unit or of one of its members.

2. Keep in mind that intense emotions and dramatic behavior tend to frighten children. They are unsure whether they are the cause of them. So as much as possible, stay calm. Don't over-react to what *might* happen. Deal only with what has happened or is happening. Speak softly.

3. Provide your child a model for how best to deal with the problem. Remember, every childhood experience is a learning experience.

4. Take the time to explain what is happening to your child, and then interpret what it will mean for him and the family. A child with few life experiences cannot be expected to understand and comprehend everything that occurs around him. If left to his own interpretation of what has occurred, se-rious emotional damage may result because a child invariably will attempt to understand what has happened in terms of something he did or said that was wrong, or perhaps something he was supposed to do and failed to do. He will blame himself for the family's problems. You must not allow him to do this.

5. Point out to your child that most crises aren't as bad as they first appear and usually don't last long. Assure him that solutions are available and that you're in control of the situa-tion. Whether you're sure of it or not at the time, assure your child that everything will be all right. Children need the comfort and reassurance these words bring. In reality, most family crises are temporary and do result in satisfactory solutions.

6. When the crisis will bring certain and perhaps permanent change, explain to the child what these changes will be. Then turn your attention and his to all the things that will remain the same.

Several years ago when a friend was faced with the specter of an impending divorce, the responsibility for telling his two chil-dren fell to him. After some planning, he took them on a week-end camping trip. Before dinner that first night, he told them their mother and father were getting a divorce. The children's initial reaction was predictable: fear and panic. But before they were allowed to overreact to what they thought this meant, he made an effort to tell them exactly what it did mean. It meant their mother and father would no longer live together in the same house. Now, instead of having one home, they would have two. This, he assured them, was the only thing that would change. Then he spent a much longer time talking about all the things that were going to remain the same. Their mother would always love them and be their mother. He would always love them and be their father. They would still have to do their chores. They would still have to go to school and to do their homework. They would still have to feed the dog. They would still have to go to bed at nine o'clock. And on and on. He told me later of the relief he saw in their faces. When children know what to expect, there is little for them to fear. It's hard enough being partly responsible for such dramatic change in their young lives without making it worse by not helping the children understand and cope with it.

Are you wondering why my friend told them before supper? There was a reason. He knew the intense emotions caused by what he had to tell them would need a physical outlet. Channeling those feelings into something constructive and purposeful they all could do together had great healing value. It also gave him an opportunity to prove what he had said about things not changing. Just like always, he assigned them each a task in preparing the meal. Then, as usual, they set the table and washed the dishes. They went about the evening—just like always.

Focusing attention on the continuity of life and making sure family routines are pursued as at all other times help restore a sense of security and trust in children that can carry them successfully through crises without lasting emotional damage.

Most family crises are invitations to change. They're opportunities to bring about good and positive changes that will improve the quality of family life. They're opportunities for growth and learning, chances to get to know and trust one another better and to strengthen family relationships.

Whether family crises help or hurt our children will depend largely on our desire and ability to parent effectively in the midst of them.

Inconsistent Parental Responses

Initially, you and your child are strangers. You are as unknown to each other as strangers meeting for the first time on the street. For most of us, there's a "getting acquainted" period that may last as long as two or three years. During this time, we must get to know our children, and they us, well enough to be able to interact successfully, to get along with one another, and to live together in harmony.

The meshing of unique personalities into a workable relationship in the family is no easy task. It often takes great skill, patience, commitment, and a desire more powerful and compelling than our fears and inadequacies. The high divorce rate in our society is evidence of just how difficult it can be to integrate two carefully selected people into a family unit. The inclusion of an infant into the ongoing life of the family can be even more difficult.

Getting acquainted begins at the behavioral level. It begins by learning that certain acts directed toward the other person will result in a desired response. When a smile, for example, results in a returned smile, when an attempt to communicate is welcomed rather than rejected, or when approaching a person doesn't cause him to move away, a relationship has been established and the process of getting acquainted has begun.

The initial success of any parent-child relationship depends largely on how many of the behavioral characteristics the child exhibits that the parents consider desirable or essential. Children who meet early parental expectations tend to be accepted more quickly into the family and with more warmth and attention. It's easier for most parents, for example, to accept a child who is cuddly and responsive than it is to accept a child who doesn't like to be cuddled and pushes his parents away.

From the very beginning, the greatest challenge for most children is meeting parental expectations—being, doing, saying what their parents want and expect. For many children, being loved and accepted into the family depends on their ability to please their parents and keep them pleased.

21

*Children tend to become what their parents
expect them to be. They try to win parental
love and acceptance
by living up to the images
projected for them.*

Unless told, the only way a child can learn what pleases a parent is through the painful process of trial and error. This process can be painful because error is often punished. How can a child learn, for example, which articles in the home are toys and can be touched and which are not toys and are off limits? In the mind of a young child, they are all the same: objects of great curiosity.

The child learns what to touch and what not to touch by touching and waiting for the parental response. If the response is positive, the child learns touching that particular object is acceptable. If the parental response is negative, however, the child learns that object should not be touched.

Consider for a moment what would happen to your child if it were acceptable to touch a lamp in the living room one day but not the next. What if you praised your child one time and punished him the next for doing the same thing? What would your child be likely to think? to feel?

Most likely your child would develop into a nervous wreck, never knowing whether he would be praised or punished. Such inconsistency would cause great emotional distress, not to mention great mental confusion. He would be unsure from one moment to the next whether the act pleased or displeased you. Living in such an unpredictable environment would not be emotionally healthy or conducive to normal growth and development.

For all these reasons, it's essential that you be as clear and as consistent in your responses to your child as possible. If his picking up the living room without being told to motivates you to praise your child and give him some special attention, then make sure that one way he can *always* get praise and attention from you is by picking up the living room without being told to. Particularly with small children, if it's a no-no to touch a vase today, make sure it's a no-no to touch the same vase tomorrow and the day after. Children learn best through repetition. If the same behavior results in the same response from you every time, your child will learn both the limits and the possibilities of your relationship. He will also learn what he must do to fit in and be accepted in the family and the world around him.

Not Enough Change

When was the last time you loaded the family into the car and drove cross-country on vacation? If it's been fairly recently, you must remember well the effects that long hours of sitting in the car can have on children! Since everyone starts out filled with excitement and energy, the first couple of hours go fine. Everyone feels good and is cooperative. But then what happens? The conversation begins to lag, everyone tires of singing the same songs over and over, the constantly changing scenery outside becomes a blur of sameness and loses its interest, and no one wants to play the "I Spy" or "Alphabet" game anymore. Boredom and emotional fatigue begin to set in. This is when things start to get rough.

Children aren't by nature physically and emotionally passive. They tend to be incredibly curious and anxious to be doing something. When boredom combines with physical inertia, which results in a build-up of unreleased energy, their attitudes begin to change. Excitement is replaced by apathy, anticipation by dread. What began as fun suddenly becomes drudgery. They become physically and emotionally uncomfortable. They begin to find reasons to be unhappy. The car is too hot, they can't sleep, brother or sister isn't giving them enough room in the back seat, they need another bathroom stop, and so it goes, seemingly without end.

23

Bored people tend to become hypersensitive and hyper-critical. Little things begin to irritate and annoy them, things that would have been insignificant under normal conditions. They begin to overreact to things that are said and done. They may lash out or strike back in retaliation. Some conflicts may even be initiated between siblings just to break the boredom.

Families who travel long distances frequently with their children learn quickly the value of stopping often for rest, refreshments, and recreation for the kids. Just a few minutes of walking or running around outside the car can work miracles with unhappy passengers on a trip.

Children need stimulation. Deprived of it, they often will seek their own. With limited resources available, this could result in great distress for the entire family.

Just as too much change can overwhelm a child and cause him panic, then, not enough change in the life of a child can create its own problems. Consider what happened to Janie. I met her for the first time when she was thirteen. Though she was slightly overweight, I remember thinking how attractive she could be with a little effort. Her hair was shoulder length and hung lifeless around her face. She wore no make-up. Her clothes were plain, simple, and colorless. She was a most unimpressive sight. There was really nothing about her to catch your eye and hold your attention as your eyes might sweep the room. Quite frankly, Janie looked boring. *How odd this is,* I thought, *for a thirteen year old.*

After spending some time with Janie, I came more and more to understand why she looked and behaved the way she did. I began to understand why she tried to take her own life.

Janie was the only child of a quiet, introverted couple who lived middle-class lives in a middle-class neighborhood. Both parents enjoyed reading and working in the yard and spent most of their free time pursuing one activity or the other. Apart from their jobs and the necessary household shopping, neither parent ever found much reason for leaving the comfort and security of the home. Only on very rare occasions did they attempt to socialize with other people. They did not belong to a church or a group that would involve them in the community or activities outside the home. They really had no outside interests. They had their home and each other, and that was enough for them. After talking with them, I was impressed by how contented they seemed to be with the world they had created for themselves.

Because of the life her parents provided her, Janie grew up in a secluded, withdrawn, and extremely private world. At school she was considered a bookworm, too involved in her reading and studies to be involved in anything else. Like her parents, Janie made no effort to socialize with her peers. To everyone else, she appeared to be a loner, apparently self-sufficient and needing no one else.

The truth of the matter, however, is that Janie *did* need other people—desperately. Hardly a day passed when she did not find herself aching inside for the fantasy she played out in her mind of a close friend to become a reality. How she envied those around her who were happy, had fun, and had friends! Janie would have given almost anything to be one of them, or to have even one close friend to talk to and spend time together doing enjoyable things.

But Janie didn't know how to be like the other young people her age. She felt so different from them, like a freak, she told me. She had spent so little time socializing with other people that she hadn't mastered any of the skills. She was afraid to try anything that might attract their attention because then she would be on the spot and would only show everybody how "stupid" she really was by being inadequate. At least this way, she said, everybody thought she was a "brain." That was something—better than being ignored totally.

Deprived of friends and the fun, excitement, and stimulation those relationships might bring, Janie lived an utterly boring life. Although she excelled academically, she would have gladly traded her grades for someone with whom she could talk. Her life was so boring that she suffered from chronic depression. Emotionally, she felt weighted down with her own lifelessness. She became listless, unresponsive, and apathetic.

Then one day Janie came to realize that neither her parents nor anyone else was going to rescue her from her stagnancy. Her life would remain the same forever, she thought, unless she did something about it. The thought of having to live the rest of her life as she had lived the first thirteen years filled her with an awful dread more powerful than her desire to live.

It was at this point that Janie took charge of her life and decided to make something happen, something that would give her the attention and relief she desperately needed. One night in her room, while deeply depressed and overwhelmed by her own inadequacy as a person and the incredible loneliness that can bring, Janie tried to take her own life.

This is an extreme, dramatic example of what can happen to children—or to anybody for that matter—who stagnate helplessly in boring lives where there is little or no change. All human beings, but especially children, need the stimulation that comes from having new experiences, meeting new people, facing new challenges, or even just doing the same thing as before, but differently! Learning and growth occur in the midst of change.

Like Janie, bored children tend to withdraw into apathy, feeling lifeless or fatigued, or else they attempt to create their own excitement. Given their limited knowledge, experience, and resources, the kinds of things children often turn to for stimulation may not be approved of by their parents or society. They can easily, and quite commonly do, become involved in activities that challenge and stimulate but that also seriously threaten their health and welfare. Some of these children may become daredevils, willing to take high personal risks simply for the thrill of it. This, of course, can be dangerous, if not deadly.

Apathetic children, on the other hand, may become so dispirited, so disinterested in life and other people that they literally atrophy, with serious social, emotional, and learning disabilities resulting. Unchallenged, uninvolved children do not grow and develop normally. They do not mature at a normal pace or in normal ways. The problems their abnormal development will cause can jeopardize the rest of their lives.

26

Change Parents Can Stimulate

Children don't have to be bored. There are many more reasons for not being bored than there are for being bored. With a little effort, kids can be taught to seek out life's exciting adventures and interest themselves in what is going on around them. They can be taught to seek the good in all things rather than the bad. They can be shown how to look for what's right about themselves, other people, and the world around them rather than for what's wrong.

A positive mental attitude is essential for the emotional health and development of children. It's important that you raise your child to be an optimist instead of a pessimist. Optimists tend to be happier, healthier people, with fewer physical and emotional problems, and consequently they live longer. Their lives tend to be a joy rather than a burden. Children with positive mental attitudes *live life*. Those with negative mental attitudes merely survive.

One way to tell an optimist from a pessimist is to place a glass in front of two people and fill it halfway with water. The pessimist will see a glass that's half empty, but the optimist will see a glass that's half full.

There are some things you can do to help bring needed change and stimulation into the lives of your children if you believe they're bored and stagnant.

1. Be careful not to criticize them for their inactivity. Always avoid "oughts" and "shoulds" when discussing the problem with them. Rarely does that approach motivate. More often, it creates unneeded guilt. Far more helpful is a positive approach to the problem.

2. Remember the domino effect. Initiating one change may create its own momentum and stimulate other changes in a sequence.

3. Begin by making a change in their physical environment. Rearrange their bedrooms (with their permission). Hang a picture. Line one wall with butcher paper and invite them to create an art mural Or have two children change rooms, if possible

Sometimes such a minor change in the life of a child is all it takes to keep him emotionally and physically active for days. Other possibilities are to rearrange the furniture in other parts of the house, or place an obstruction in the middle of a normal pathway to the bathroom, kitchen, or front door, such as a balancing beam laid flat on the floor, a box, or a chair. Anything will do if it interrupts the flow of traffic and breaks the routine.

4. Then begin to make a change in their emotional environment. Happy children are those who are emotionally invested in something more important than their own wants, needs, or inadequacies. It could be a building or a gardening project, a sewing class, a paper route, or Girl or Boy Scouts. Other possibilities include a project to feed the hungry or clothe those unfortunates in your town who need help, or some service for the elderly. The point is that children busy thinking of ways to help others are rarely bored with themselves.

5. Offer changes in their mental environment. Take routine trips to the library. Encourage them to read. Include them in family decision-making. Challenge their minds with a problem to solve, such as how best to rearrange a room or lay out a rock garden. Encourage them to plan and execute a recreation program for other children in the neighborhood. There are many possibilities.

6. Challenge their imaginations with "What if . . ." games. What if I were president? What if I had all the money in the world? What if we lived on the moon? Not only do such games stimulate your children's natural curiosity and creativity, but they also open a world of infinite possibilities for them. It has been said that what characterizes great persons more than anything else is a vivid imagination.

7. Find a way to get your children physically active. Enroll them in an athletic program, a dance class, an exercise class— anything that will *get them moving*. Lots of physical exercise is essential for the healthy development of children. Children on the move don't stagnate; children busy doing something are rarely bored.

It's important that you keep your children stimulated by new experiences, new challenges, and new opportunities to learn and do. Active, involved children tend to remain committed to life and themselves. They don't become apathetic and careless. Through active involvement, their lives remain interesting and worthy of pursuit, and their self-esteem is enhanced.

Recognizing Symptoms of Stress in Your Child

The alert, attentive parent can often tell when his child is experiencing too much or too little change. Too much stress tends to result in certain kinds of coping behavior in children, while not enough results in other kinds. Assuming there is no organic or medical reason for the behavior, the following types of behavior can be clear signals of distress in your child.

Too Much Change

General irritability. Remember the last time you took your child to the state fair? All day long he was bombarded with sights, sounds, rides, and excitement. It was lots of fun—at least until everyone got in the car for the ride home. Then what happened? Your child suddenly became very tired, grumpy, and irritable. Right?

Inability to concentrate. Too much change going on around a child causes distractions. Distracted children have a difficult time focusing their attention on any one thing for very long.

Hyperactivity. Overstimulated children tend to move and talk a great deal. The stimulation creates stress that must find a physical outlet. Hyperactivity is one way some children try to cope with too much change in their lives.

Nervous laughter or tics. Laughter is an effective stress-relieving mechanism that most people use from time to time. Nervous laughter in children is a clear sign of distress. Sometimes this distress will be expressed physically as a nervous tic, usually in the face.

Stuttering. Some children experiencing high levels of stress from too much change in their lives will become so tense and distressed that they have difficulty putting thoughts and feelings into words. They may stutter.

Nightmares. Many children overwhelmed by too much change will feel helpless and out of control. Their feelings of personal vulnerability may be expressed through nightmares.

Being accident prone. Sometimes children preoccupied with trying to cope with too much change around them will become careless. They may pay less and less attention to how they look and how they do things. The result can be that they appear accident prone.

Not Enough Change

Boredom and lethargy. Bored and lethargic children tend to be those who are not being stimulated and challenged. They can find nothing to attract and hold their attention.

Fatigue. Inactivity in children tends to breed fatigue. They seem to feel tired most of the time and want to sleep more than usual.

Insomnia. Understimulated children tend to have trouble sleeping through the night, although they usually sleep some during the day and get far more sleep than they need.

Loss of appetite. Children experiencing stagnation tend to lose interest in most activities, even such mundane things as eating. They may become disinterested in most other family functions, too.

Loss of pleasure capacity. Bored children do not have fun. They find nothing to laugh and smile about. Their worlds become oppressively dull. They have a hard time enjoying anything.

Hypochondria. Understressed children tend to find many physical things wrong with themselves. They believe themselves to be ill with unusual frequency.

Depression. Children not experiencing enough stimulation in their lives tend to be depressed. Their moods are often gloomy and despairing, and they move as though weighted down with a great burden. They have little energy.

Points to Remember

1. Life is a constantly unfolding revelation. Each day brings change—lots of it!

2. All change causes physical and emotional stress. Stress results from our attempt to keep internal conditions stable and constant despite changing conditions around us.

3. Some changes cause more distress than others. The changes that cause the most trouble are those that threaten what we consider most important.

4. It is the extremes of not enough or too much change that are most harmful to children. Too much overwhelms them, while not enough results in boredom.

5. An optimum level of change is enough to challenge and stimulate without overwhelming and defeating. A healthy balance will enhance the functioning of a child rather than inhibit it.

6. Healthy, well-adjusted children tend to grow into healthy, well-adjusted adults.

Chapter 2

. . . But Words Can Never Hurt Me?

It was a Saturday morning, but not just any Saturday morning. This one was different! My six-year-old son and I had been preparing for this day for weeks. Both of us were so nervous about it that we didn't sleep well the night before. Both of us were up early. Jonathan tried to lose himself in the morning cartoons while I busied myself with paperwork in my study. Our efforts failed. We soon found ourselves sitting across from each other at the table.

"What if I mess up?" his young, untried voice cried out to me in genuine concern. It was hard to tell at that moment whether his eagerness or his fear was stronger.

"You'll do fine, son!" I assured him with a smile I hoped would appear as sincere as his concern. "Just remember what you've learned these past six weeks. Do what they tell you, and everything will be fine."

Apparently, I was less than convincing. My son wasn't satisfied. I could tell his mind was filling with disasters only his imagination could make real.

"But, what if . . . ," he said over and over again, each time offering a new possibility. He was working himself into a real panic.

"Son, if you make a mistake, well, don't worry about it. Everybody makes mistakes," I said. "Just go out there and do your best. And have fun!"

That seemed to help. Some. At last it was time to channel all his nervous energy into physical activity. It was time to go. I could feel his excitement mounting as we neared the ballpark. The car had barely stopped rolling when he burst out the door and ran headlong to join his teammates already warming up on the field. As I watched him dash through the crowd with his baseball cap askew on his head and his baggy pants flapping around his legs, I had no idea that this was the start of something that would consume the next twelve years of his life.

This was his first baseball game. It was his first organized competition of any sort. He had been drafted by a pony league team that most people in the know considered a legitimate title contender that year. They had some good speed and some "big sticks," as the saying goes. But they were opening against the other team in the league considered to be a title contender. The game was attracting a lot of interest from spectators at the park.

Settling myself as comfortably as possible on the highest level of the wooden bleachers amidst the other excited parents, I didn't have to wait long for the game to start.

"Play ball!" shouted the umpire behind the plate as he donned his mask and chest protector.

I watched eagerly as Jonathan's team took to the field. He was not among the faces I could barely recognize under the caps pulled low over the eyes. He was one of the three boys still sitting on the bench. I knew he would get to play, though, because it was a league rule that every boy play at least one inning of each game.

33

It was an exciting game! The score seesawed as one team would get the lead and lose it again. Jonathan's team was trailing by two runs as they came to bat in the bottom of the last inning. They had to score two runs to send the game into extra innings or three runs to win. Jonathan was still sitting on the bench.

Our first batter grounded out on a slow roller to the pitcher. Our next batter drew a walk. Suddenly, I found my heart pounding fiercely in my throat as the next scheduled batter was called back to the dugout and Jonathan was sent to bat in his place. I watched in frozen panic as he made his way slowly to the batter's box in front of the opposing team's catcher and the home plate umpire. If I had not almost fallen off the bleachers from trying to get a better view, I think I might have passed out from holding my breath!

The first pitch was wild and went scooting all the way to the backstop. Our runner on first advanced to second base. Jonathan represented the tying run. There was one out. The next pitch was high. Ball two.

"A walk's as good as a hit!" I heard myself yell above the noise of the tense and anxious crowd. "Just two more balls, son, and you're safe on first with a walk," I whispered silently. "Please don't blow it!"

The next pitch would have been a ball because it was a little high and out of the strike zone. But the groan that sprang into the throats of the crowd as they watched his bat begin its long sweep around exploded into a cheer a split second later as the ball went sailing over the first baseman's head into right field. Jonathan had a stand-up double! The runner already on base scored. We were now just one run down. I watched with great pride and relief as his eyes searched me out of the crowd in the bleachers. Once he found me, he flashed me one of the biggest smiles I had ever seen.

After a moment, the stands grew tense and silent again. Our next batter approached the plate. All eyes were now focused on him as they had been on Jonathan a moment before.

The first pitch was fouled off. Then, out of nowhere, just as the pitcher was starting his next wind-up, the crowd was hushed by a mournful wailing coming from second base. It could be heard all over the ballpark! As my eyes followed all the others to second base, I saw my son sitting down on the base, his head buried in his arms resting on his knees in front of him. He was crying his heart out!

Afraid he had been hurt, several coaches and umpires raced to his side. The crowd was so quiet we all could hear his coach speak to him.

"What's wrong, Jonathan?" he asked.

Then it came. A message from my son to me and every other parent raising young children.

"I'm scared," he wailed amidst sobs. "I don't know what to do!"

The Importance of Communication

People communicate. Every day and in every way, all human interaction involves an exchange of thoughts and feelings. What is not said is sometimes as important as what *is* said. The smile on my son's face as he stood proudly at second base told me more than words could possibly have expressed. His unexpected behavior of sitting down on the base instead of standing ready to run gave me and everyone else watching a message quite different from that of the smile. Burying his face in his arms gave us yet another message. Then there was his crying. Finally, who could mistake the fear of making a mistake that might cost his team the game that underlined his words? Every human action involves communication. We communicate even in our silence.

Effective communication is an essential part of any healthy relationship. Living and working together would not be possible without it. It is our primary problem-solving tool. Healing in bruised and broken lives would be less likely without it. It is an important expression of all sharing and caring. The ability to communicate is also a primary source of distress in troubled minds and relationships.

This morning was one of "those" mornings in my house. Know the kind I mean? Every parent does! Just in the one hour before my kids left for school, I had to serve as policeman, judge, jury, social worker, mental health therapist, cook, house-parent, manager, and taxi driver!

It began with a breakfast eaten on the run because we were behind schedule. Competing with hairdryers and some radio disc jockey saying what a rotten day it was, we went through a check list to make sure they had all they needed for their day at school and a field trip. In the midst of all this, my daughter was desperately trying to express her frustration over an unusually difficult science project while my son was wanting to know if a friend could spend the night. Finally ready, we made a mad sprint to the car where a disagreement erupted immediately between my son and daughter over who would ride in the front seat and who would be in the back. Whew! What a relief it was for me to drop them off at school and then go to work!

Mornings like this remind me that raising children requires many skills, not to mention patience, compassion, wisdom, and determination. But no skill is as important as communication. Strong, healthy families do not exist without good communication.

Communication is the primary vehicle of teaching and learning. Through communication with parents and other important adults in their lives, our children learn all they know about the world in which they live, about the people who occupy it and, most important, about themselves—who and what they are as people.

Some parents teach their children that the world is a hostile and dangerous place, filled with uncertainty and forces over which they have no control. Other children learn that the world is a wonderful, exciting place, an ever-expanding playground filled with magical possibilities.

Some parents teach their children to fear people. These children tend to grow up believing people are basically bad and untrustworthy. They become reluctant to establish meaningful relationships. Still other children are taught life's vital purpose and deepest meaning is to be found in healthy relationships with other people.

Of even more concern, many children are taught by parents and other adults that childhood is an inferior condition that must be outgrown. It is what children do while they are waiting to grow up. The more fortunate children are those who are taught they are images of the Creator, their bodies meant to be a temple of the Spirit, their minds an unlimited universe of possibilities, their lives a miracle more precious than anything else imaginable. The parents of these children understand childhood as being an important time in every human life, a time to be protected and preserved in order to allow maximum growth and development.

Children learn these and all things through communication with their parents and other adults. Young children tend to believe what they are told. They have no reason to doubt it. If you tell your children they are bad and deserving of punishment, it is likely they will believe you. Children tend to become what their parents expect them to be because they try to live up to the image projected for them.

Communication can be a building tool or a weapon of destruction. It can build character or assassinate it. It can strengthen a relationship, a dream, a commitment, or it can weaken it through erosion until it collapses. It can challenge a mind to reach beyond itself to encompass a possibility outside its understanding, or it can overwhelm the same mind with its inadequacy. Communication can clarify reality or distort it, shape a personality or disfigure it. It can overflow a life with joy and happiness or fill it with unspeakable misery and suffering.

Spoken and Unspoken Communication

Parents communicate with their children both verbally and nonverbally. The words "I love you" communicate something very special. Kids need to hear them. A lot! But a long, affectionate hug is likely to communicate the same thing—even more so. And combining the words with a hug communicates a still deeper message. The words tell children they are loved. The hug shows it. The hug interprets the meaning of the words in a way that children can easily understand and appreciate.

It's important to the emotional health of your children that they not only believe they're loved because they've heard you say it, but because they *feel* loved as well. Beliefs are taught most often through words. Feelings are experienced through behavior. Children who have been told they are loved but do not feel loved tend to have emotional problems.

Children need to know they are loved as well as feel *loved. One without the other can handicap a child with uncertainty.*

Without adults' mastery of language, children may find words to be terribly ambiguous and confusing. Most often, they must seek the meaning of the words in the parent's behavior that accompanies them. The word "no" is likely to be better understood and taken more seriously if it is accompanied by a scowling face reflecting parental displeasure rather than a warm, relaxed smile. To be effective communication, words must be backed by parental behavior that reinforces their meaning or purpose.

If the parental behavior accompanying the words does not clarify their meaning, children may turn to past experiences in similar situations for their meaning. When the words "I love you," for example, are always accompanied by an affectionate hug, a child learns a particular meaning for them, a meaning that inspires trust and security because they make the child feel good and do not change.

But when the same words are accompanied by parental behavior that hurts instead of feels good, the words take on quite a different meaning. Reinforcing the words "I love you" with a hug tells a child one thing. Reinforcing them with discipline given in anger tells him something different. In both cases the child is likely to believe he's loved because he's been told he is and has no reason to disbelieve the parent. But hugs help the child feel good and worthy of love. Harsh discipline, on the other hand, causes the child to feel bad and unworthy of love.

When the words "I love you" accompany both hugs and excessive discipline, they take on a double meaning, depending on the situation and the mood of the parent. *Double-message communication* causes confusion and conflict within the child. It's difficult for young children to know with certainty which meaning of love will be applied in unfamiliar situations, such as times of family crisis, tragedy, or great stress. They're unsure whether to expect a hug or anger.

All children want their parents to love them. They want, need, and strive for hugs. But most children don't want or strive for physical discipline. Yet, if love means both, how is the child to achieve one while avoiding the other? The resulting conflict in the child is similar to that caused when the same hand is used both to caress and hit. It won't take the child long to learn to duck out of the way in order to avoid the hand, whether it's offering a caress or delivering a blow. The emotional conflict in the child derives from the desire and need to receive love and the fear of getting it.

Vague, *unclear communication* is another form of interaction between you and your child that can result in great distress for your child and displeasure for you. Consider the command so well known by all of us who are parents: "You behave!"

At first glance this command may appear clear and direct. In most situations familiar to children, it might be. But not always. There are times when we put our children in situations where they are not sure what it means to behave. Behaving in the back yard while at play, for example, is something quite different from behaving at the dinner table with company present, isn't it? And certainly, behaving on the football field means something different from behaving in the grocery store! There is "appropriate" behavior for almost every situation. Teaching our children how to behave involves teaching them appropriate behavior for every situation.

Expecting our children to behave means we have certain expectations they must meet in order to please us. When our children don't live up to our behavioral expectations, we often react as though they are being willfully disobedient or rebellious or are seeking revenge on us for something we did or didn't do that displeased them. Our tendency is to react with anger and frustration and to feel justified in punishing them.

The mistake many of us make in this regard is that we don't spell out precisely what we expect of our children in new and different situations. Instead, we sometimes just turn them loose with that command to behave and leave them to discover for themselves what it means. The result is often disappointment for us and punishment for them.

A similar predicament would exist for you if you showed up for your new job and were simply told by your employer, "Get to work!" Most adults would panic in such a situation, totally unsure of what was expected of them. You would want a job description, something that would clearly tell you what was expected.

Double-message communication and unclear communication set children up to fail rather than succeed. Children cannot live up to our expectations unless they know precisely what those expectations are.

What we do inadvertently in such situations is *set our children up to fail*. We don't equip them with the necessary knowledge, skills, and understanding to succeed—that is, to live up to our expectations. Children who chronically fall short of their parents' expectations are taught a very important lesson—how to fail. And teaching children how to fail has the eventual effect of convincing them they don't have what it takes to succeed.

Guidelines for Effective Communication

It's very important that you communicate clearly and effectively with your child, particularly in those areas where you expect certain responses from him. A child cannot live up to adult expectations unless he knows beforehand exactly what those expectations are.

Perhaps the following suggestions will help you be a more effective communicator with your child:

1. Always use language a child can understand. Don't try to improve language and vocabulary skills while giving an order. Keep your language simple and direct.

2. If possible, get at or below eye level with the child and look him in the eye while you speak. Children live in a world bombarded constantly with words and phrases, many of which they must tune out because they don't understand them. By speaking directly to the child, you not only get and hold his attention, but your behavior also tells him that what you have to say is important.

3. Always talk slowly, softly, and clearly. Have you ever noticed how an upset child will often calm down if you whisper? The reason is that he has to calm down if he wants to hear what's being said.

4. Explain to the child what is occurring and exactly what you expect from him. Spell it out! For example, the first time I took my children to the grocery store with me, I told them where we were going and why. Then I went through an entire litany of okay and not-okay behavior: it's okay to talk, but it's not okay to shout; it's okay to walk, but it's not okay to run; it's okay to look, but it's not okay to touch.

5. Make sure your expectations are reasonable and appropriate for the child's age. *Don't expect your child never to make a mistake or always to behave exactly as you want him to.* Chil-

dren are human beings, not robots we can program. Be sure to set your child up to succeed, not fail.

6. Ask the child if he understands what you expect from him. Ask if he has any questions. It's sometimes helpful to have a child repeat back what you have said to make sure what you said is what he heard!

7. Be consistent in the words you use and the behavior that accompanies them. Be sure your words and behavior complement each other, define each other, and really mean what you intend them to mean. Avoid double-message communication.

8. Reward your child's efforts at listening and then attempting to do what you have asked him to do. Children desperately need parental acceptance and approval. They will do practically anything to get it. Even behave!

Actions Speak Louder Than Words!

If you live in my neighborhood, you know that my wife is one of those people who never leave any doubt in anyone's mind about whether they're angry. She doesn't get angry often, but when she does, I and half the county know it! But we don't find out the way you might think. She doesn't yell and scream like most people. No, such a simple, direct approach would be too easy! Her style is more imaginative. My wife stomps around the house and slams doors. I don't mean she shuts them loudly. She slams them! She particularly likes cabinet doors in the kitchen, which tend to bounce right back open so she can slam them again!

Several times throughout the years, I have found the courage to approach her at these times to inquire into what has upset her so much. Invariably, she turns to me with something on her face that once may have remotely resembled a smile, and in a voice I know would melt butter she assures me there's nothing wrong and she's not the least bit angry. No sooner do I turn my back, however, than a picture on the wall in my study crashes to the floor from a cabinet door's being slammed in the kitchen.

Obviously, my wife is telling me one thing with her words and something quite different with her behavior. Is there any doubt which speaks louder to me? Despite her words to the contrary, her behavior convinces me she is angry. As I said earlier, we're always communicating, even when we don't say a word.

Most parents tend to relate more to a child's behavior than to the child himself. More of their attention is focused on what the child does or does not do than on what the child thinks or feels about whatever it was he did or didn't do. And most parents react to the child at a behavioral level because it is the behavior of the child that is pleasing or displeasing, good or bad. Parents perceive the child's behavior as the problem because it is what's causing them the discomfort, embarrassment, or frustration. Correcting the problem, then, means changing the child's behavior. What most parents overlook, however, is that the problem for the child is not his behavior but the thinking or the feeling behind it. An infant crying in his crib, for example, most likely needs to be fed, to have a diaper changed, or to feel the warmth and security of Mother's arms. But it is the crying that bothers Mother and motivates her to action. The problem for her is how best to get the child to stop crying. The problem for the child, however, is not the crying but the hunger he feels and how best to get Mother to feed him.

Like my wife's slamming doors when angry and an infant's crying when hungry, all human behavior is a form of communication. It's telling us something important and specific about what the person is thinking or feeling. Thus, for you to understand why your child is behaving the way he is, you must first discover the feelings and thinking behind the behavior. There is a reason for all human behavior. My wife slams doors because she's angry. The infant cries because he's hungry.

The message my wife's slamming doors gives me is that something is wrong. It tells me there's a problem of some kind somewhere that has her very upset. Whether she has a right to be upset is anybody's guess. The fact facing me is that she is.

When my wife gets angry, I have a choice in terms of how to deal with the situation. I can ignore it and hope it goes away. I can try to control it by punishing it. Or I can try to relieve the anger by solving the problem.

Which of the three approaches I take will be determined by how I perceive her behavior. If I see what is happening to her as unimportant or just a tantrum from a spoiled child, I am likely to treat it as though it's not important and just ignore it. On the other hand, if I perceive her behavior as rebellious, defiant, or an intentional effort to hurt or get even with me, I am more likely to try to control it with punishment. Finally, if I understand her behavior to be a symptom of an emotional problem and a cry for help, I am likely to try to find out what the problem is and solve it.

Transferring this understanding to your relationship with your children, I trust you would never intentionally ignore their attempts to get your attention. And controlling their behavior with punishment does not usually solve the problem that is its cause either. It may relieve your discomfort, but rarely does it settle the underlying conflict. The problem continues and will likely show itself in some other form of undesirable behavior. Getting the infant to quit crying without feeding him, for example, will relieve Mother's problem, but it doesn't meet the child's need that prompted the crying.

Simply reacting to a child's behavior without concern for the thinking and the feeling behind it is a form of negative communication. You are nonverbally telling the child one of several things:

- The child is not worth your special interest and concern.
- The child's problem is not very important.
- The effect of the child's behavior on you or others is more important than whatever is bothering the child.
- You do not care enough to try to understand him.
- The child is the problem.

Children who come to believe they're problems are likely to be just that; children are self-fulfilling prophecies.

The verbal and nonverbal communication between you and your child can impart positive thoughts and feelings that enhance the relationship and your child's self-esteem, or negative thoughts and feelings that threaten the relationship and damage your child's self-esteem. Any communication that tells your child he is loved, wanted, accepted, and worthy is positive and is likely to result in positive attitudes and behavior in your child. Conversely, communication that tells your child he is bad, inadequate, unlovable, and unworthy is negative and will probably result in his acting out his guilt and pain in behavior you find unacceptable and perhaps intolerable.

The verbal and nonverbal communication between you and your child can impart positive thoughts and feelings that enhance the relationship and your child's self-esteem, or negative thoughts and feelings that threaten the relationship and damage your child's self-esteem.

Actions do speak louder than words. Ask my wife! She knows how to get my attention when words fail. So do children. Children learn more from what we do than from what we say. A parent who adopts a "Do as I say, not as I do" style of parenting is only fooling himself. In more ways than many of us want to acknowledge, our children tend to grow up to be just like us.

Verbal Communication That Can Hurt

Sometimes we parents say things to our children that hurt rather than help, things that often accomplish the opposite of what was intended. Some parents go so far as to attack and wound their children with words intentionally. But most do so accidentally. We all say and do things in times of crisis, great stress, and anger that we really don't mean and later regret.

If sticks and stones can break bones, parents must be aware that words can do even more harm. It is just as possible to assault a child emotionally with words as it is possible to assault a child physically with sticks and stones. Whereas physical wounds may heal, emotional wounds usually do not heal so quickly or so well. The scars they leave often inhibit the child's growth, learning, and development.

If sticks and stones can break bones, words can do even more harm. Emotional scars can handicap a child for life.

Most damaging to a child are repeated emotional hurts. Just as a bruise on your arm won't heal so long as it's being exposed to more blows, so emotional bruises won't heal when they're constantly being rebruised. It's also less likely these wounds will heal if they're ignored. A broken arm won't heal properly unless it's set straight. Similarly, a broken heart may not heal properly unless it, too, is set straight. Healing involves care and nurturing.

Consider the following situation: Knowing Mother is upset because of an unresolved argument with Father, five-year-old Sally tries to help by setting the table while Mother is preparing dinner. Sally feels good about what she's doing because Mother seems pleased and appreciative. Sally is trying to follow Mother's instructions precisely. Everything is going fine. But then, disaster strikes! A glass Sally is carrying to the table slips from her tiny hands and shatters into a hundred pieces on the floor. Devastated, Sally begins to cry. This is the last straw for Mother. She explodes in a rage and screams at Sally for what she has done. Still raging, Mother spanks Sally while accusing her of dropping the glass intentionally. Finally, Mother sends Sally to her room crying hysterically, assuring the child she will never again be allowed to help in the kitchen.

Right or wrong, good or bad, regardless of what we might think about this incident between Sally and her mother, one thing is certain. There's nothing that can be done to change it. It happened. Mother reacted to the broken glass in a way she might not have had she not already been under so much stress. All parents lose their cool from time to time. We all occasionally say and do things we later regret. What is most important to Sally and her mother now is what happens next.

Mother can react to what has happened in such a way that the pain and suffering are maximized or minimized. If Mother reacts with guilt and shame, she is likely to become so engrossed in coping with her own feelings that she pays little or no attention to what Sally must be thinking and feeling alone in her bedroom. Leaving the emotional wounds unattended will only make matters worse for both the mother and the child.

What Sally and her mother need most is an opportunity for healing to take place not only within them, but between them. Mother needs to resolve the problem with her husband and not allow herself to become trapped in feelings of guilt for what occurred in the kitchen. Sally needs her mother to acknowledge that the broken glass was an accident and that what happened was really not her fault. Sally needs Mother's explanation, apology, and support. Mother needs Sally's understanding and forgiveness. Through such a healing process, their trust and love for each other can be deepened, their relationship enhanced, their self images restored to health, and the event in the kitchen can be forgotten as one of life's unfortunate mishaps.

It is important you remember, though, that the healing process must be initiated by you, the parent. Young children are incapable of meeting their own needs in such a situation and cannot be expected to meet yours. It's incredible how much healing can occur when such words as "I'm sorry" are applied to the situation. They are truly magic.

Just as some words bring healing, there are others that bring suffering. Any words that attack, demean, degrade, or threaten the self-image or self-esteem of a child can be damaging to the child's thinking and feeling. These words should be avoided.

The following are words and statements you should avoid using with your child. They can have an incredibly negative effect upon emotional health and development.

"You are . . ." Statements

These are character statements. They don't tell a child something important about his behavior. Instead, they reflect something important about the child as a person. Telling a child he's bad, mean, ugly, stupid, or selfish can make a normal child, experiencing normal childhood difficulties and growing pains, distort his self-perception into something abnormal.

"You always . . ." and "You never . . ." Statements

Statements by parents that begin with these words are doubly damaging to the emotional health of a child. On the one hand, *they are not true.* "Always" and "never" are absolute terms that don't recognize the reality of exceptions. No human being is always one way and never another. Children are not always good, always bad, always late, or always anything. Neither are they never helpful, never ready, never on time, never willing to please. Sometimes they are and sometimes they aren't.

These statements also reflect on the character of the child instead of on his behavior. The words imply personal inadequacy. They make the child believe there's something wrong with him, something not good enough. Most children are able to meet parental expectations at least some of the time. There's hope they can become more like what their parents want them to be. There's no such hope for the "always" and "never" kid. He is trapped within a character defect over which he has no control and which he cannot change in order to win the approval of his parents. He's doomed to his imperfect nature. Or so he's led to believe.

"Why can't you be like . . ." Statements

Comments that compare one child unfavorably with another can hurt tremendously. Again, they imply personal inadequacy and loss of parental love unless the child becomes more like someone else and less like himself. Some children are so anxious to please their parents that they will do almost anything—even denying themselves—in order to be what they think their parents want them to be. Most damaging to children is when parents compare grades, achievements, personal appearance, motivations, and abilities.

No two children are alike. Each is unique and special in his own way. It's important to the mental and emotional health of your children that you care enough to discover what makes each one special and help them develop their uniqueness rather than constantly point out how they're different from other children and wish they were someone else.

Parents who encourage competition between siblings through unfavorable comparisons are programming the younger or more inadequate child to fail. Just as children can become comfortable with success, so can they become comfortable with failure—so comfortable, in fact, that failure can become a way of life.

"You can't . . ." Statements

How many times in the life of a typical child does he hear these words? Over and over again, day after day, year after year they are repeated to children. Some children hear them so much that it's a wonder they have any self-confidence at all. The sad truth is that many of these children don't. Their lack of self-confidence shows in everything they attempt, as well as in all those things they won't even try.

There's a world of difference between telling your child "You can't" and "You may not" do this or that. The first tells the child he's incapable of doing whatever the task may be. It implies personal inadequacy. On the other hand, telling a child "No, you may not" doesn't imply personal inadequacy. It's a simple, clear message to the child that permission is not granted. That's all. It says nothing about the child's ability.

"Be a good boy/girl and . . ." Statements

Associating goodness with doing something can be a serious parental mistake. All children need to believe they're basically good and worthy of their parents' love and acceptance. But goodness is an inherent quality of human life, not something that's earned. Respect is earned, as are admiration, trust, and acceptance. But goodness is a basic quality existing in all children.

It's important that you affirm the basic nature of your child as being good, even though the child's behavior at the time may be undesirable. To make goodness conditional, dependent upon what is said and done, is to open the door to the possibility that the child is not good, bad perhaps, and therefore not deserving of love. Such a notion can have serious consequences for the emotional health and development of a child. Teaching a child he is good only as long as he does what is pleasing to you sets the stage for serious emotional conflict in the child when he makes a normal childhood mistake that brings your displeasure.

It's critical that we parents punish and reward the child's behavior, not the child. It's one thing to say to a small child who has just bitten another, "You are a bad boy!" and quite another to say, "Biting is bad!" The first tells the child something important about who and what he is as a person. The second tells the child something important about the behavior of biting other children.

Similarly, when the child apologizes to the wounded child, it's one message to the child when the parent responds by saying, "Good boy!" and quite another message when the parent rewards the desired behavior with a statement such as "Apologizing to someone you have hurt is good and the right thing to do."

Both situations teach the child something important. Whether what is learned hurts or helps the child will depend largely on whether the parent focuses attention on the basic nature of the child or the child's undesirable behavior. One can cripple, the other empower. As parents, our goal is to build up our children, not tear them down.

Such statements can also be used to manipulate a child emotionally by conveying this message: I will love you if you do what I want. It's exploitative of a child emotionally, too, in that it uses a child's need to be loved and accepted as a means of getting from the child what the parent wants. Neither situation is healthy.

Points to Remember

Many parents talk to their children or behave toward them in ways that communicate something negative about the children rather than about their behavior. Emotionally healthy parents realize their children are good gifts from God. Unacceptable *behavior* is their concern and therefore should be the focus of their attention and efforts to correct it.

Still other parents have little to say to their children unless it's a negative or critical remark or an attempt to correct them. These parents miss wonderful opportunities to praise their children, to build their self-esteem and feelings of worthiness because they're so busy looking for weaknesses in need of correction. Sadly, then, many of these children learn the only way they're going to get parental attention is to misbehave.

As a concerned and conscientious parent, you can help your children by following these simple guidelines.

1. Learn to be more positive with and about them. Focus more attention on the good that exists in them and the world around them.

2. Listen to their negative or unpleasant feelings without feeling threatened or wounded. Do not counterattack. Instead, offer guidance and understanding.

3. Recognize and affirm the best in them rather than search constantly for problems to be treated and resolved.

4. Make sure words and behavior complement each other, define each other, and truly impart the message to your children that you intend. Be clear. Be consistent.

5. Maintain a healthy, positive environment within the family, positive attitudes, positive behavior, positive interaction. Positive people are generally more successful in life and better able to cope with its ups and downs. Positive people not only retain a sense of possibility in the midst of negative experiences, but they also retain a sense of hope.

Chapter 3
What a Difference a Hug Makes!

I saw Michelle and Marlena the other day. They were playing in the front yard while their mothers sat in lounge chairs visiting nearby. This was the first time I had seen them together since they came home from the hospital sixteen months earlier. As I admired them from afar, I became amazed at how different they were from each other. The difference wasn't so much in their appearance and physical size (though Michelle was larger than Marlena), as it was in their behavior—what they were like as children. Their attitudes and personalities were strikingly unalike.

Michelle was up and running around the yard, flailing her arms wildly in circles as she ran, jumping occasionally and chattering incessantly it seemed. Once in a while she would squeal with delight as she bounced from one curious object in the yard to the next. Marlena, on the other hand, could barely walk, much less run. She still seemed terribly unsure of herself once she stood up on her wobbly legs and tried to move after Michelle, only to find herself sitting again. During most of the time I observed her, Marlena sat quietly on the blanket, toying absent-mindedly with a stuffed animal and watching Michelle hop around the yard. While Michelle was excitedly looking, smelling, and touching everything she could get her hands on, Marlena seemed uninterested. She spoke very little and appeared content to play quietly alone. Several times I watched Michelle race playfully into her mother's open arms and engage in a lively exchange of chatter and hugs. But not Marlena. There was hardly any interaction between her and her mother.

From a behavioral perspective, Marlena could only be described as basically a passive child, perhaps a little slow in her social and motor development. Michelle, on the other hand, was clearly a little advanced in her development and could only be described as an active child.

I wondered then how two children born only hours apart in the same hospital on the same day and raised in families living on the same street and with similar levels of income could grow to be so different in just sixteen months. I knew, of course, that no two children are alike. I also knew that children develop at their own pace. Most physical differences between people can be explained as a result of heredity. At this point in our understanding of genetics, we can't control the color of our hair or eyes, our features, or how tall we become. These are physical traits we inherit from our parents.

But such is not the case when it comes to behavioral differences between people. In most cases, behavior is learned, not inherited. In the early months and years of life, it's learned primarily through a child's relationship with parents.

No, the differences I was observing between Michelle and Marlena were not the result of heredity. Both girls were physically healthy. Both had very adequate mental capabilities. Both children would be considered normal for their age by almost any standard.

Instead, the behavioral differences between the girls were the result of the kind of parenting they had received during the first sixteen months of their lives. The reason the girls were different was that their relationships with their mothers was different. The two women had very different approaches to raising their daughters. Their attitudes and beliefs about children and parenting were also different.

In conversations with the mothers over the next several weeks, I came to learn the following:

First, though both mothers wanted and had planned for their children, Marlena's mother perceived parenting basically as a tough and demanding job. She had watched her own mother work and struggle to raise her and her three siblings after her father died.

Michelle's mother, on the other hand, saw parenting basically as an opportunity. She believed raising children involved more good times than bad; whereas Marlena's mother looked forward to the occasional good times as her strength during the bad times.

Second, Marlena's mother had a basic fear of failing as a parent. She seemed a little confused about her role as a mother and how best to fulfill it. As a result, she relied heavily on outside information and opinions for guidance. Her basic approach to parenting was to avoid making mistakes.

Michelle's mother, however, spent her time and energy not avoiding mistakes but rather creating opportunities for her child to learn and do and become.

Marlena's mother's approach to parenting was basically passive: to let nature take its course and deal with it as it comes. Michelle's mother, on the other hand, was an active mother; she initiated activity. Are you seeing any similarities between the mothers and daughters?

Third, because of her fear of failure, Marlena's mother kept her parenting on a structured, rigid schedule. Just about everything was done by the clock. Feedings occurred every two or three hours. Diapers were changed once an hour. Naps and bedtimes were strictly enforced. Exercise was kept on schedule.

Michelle's mother was more spontaneous in her parenting. She was also more relaxed. Feedings occurred when Michelle was hungry. Diapers were changed when they were wet or messy. Naps and bedtimes were scheduled, but the schedule was flexible.

Fourth, both mothers attended prenatal parenting classes before the birth of their children. Marlena's mother joined a group that spent much of its time discussing and rehearsing the difficult and painful aspects of childbirth and parenting. The instructor believed rehearsal beforehand would diminish the difficulty in actual practice.

Michelle's mother, on the other hand, attended a class that emphasized the positive aspects of childbirth and parenting. Much of their time was spent discussing what could be done to stimulate their children physically, mentally, and emotionally to enhance their growth and development.

Fifth, Marlena's mother was cautioned over and over against spoiling the child, against allowing herself to be manipulated by the child's crying or to be controlled by her moods. She was told to be careful not to slip into emotional bondage to her child. She was taught the best way to help her child learn to go to sleep alone was to let her cry herself to sleep. She was also taught it was unwise to respond too quickly or too often to the child's cries when unrelated to physical hunger or pain. To do so could result in the child's being overly dependent, becoming spoiled, and turning Mother into a physical and emotional slave.

Although the need for parents of young children to have some time alone was discussed, the group Michelle's mother attended never talked about such things as emotional bondage, being manipulated or controlled by the child, or even spoiling the child. Instead, the instructor discussed in detail the developmental stages of early childhood, pointing out the special needs of the child at each stage, and suggesting positive, helpful ways those needs could be met. The instructor assured her not to fear the child's crying. All children cry, sometimes for no apparent reason. It's done not to manipulate the parent but merely to communicate. Michelle's mother was also taught that feeding schedules are nice, but it's more important that the child be spared the anxieties and uncertainties of hunger so early in her life. She was encouraged to respond to the child's needs immediately, without waiting for the clock. The quicker a parent responds to a child's crying, the less the child will cry. Studies have shown that children whose mothers responded quickly to their cries during the first year of life cried less after one year than children whose parents responded slowly for fear of spoiling them.

Michelle's mother also learned the value of lots and lots of physical contact. Children given lots of attention and lots of hugs from parents tend to develop faster, have higher, more advanced mental capabilities, are better adjusted, and are happier children than their counterparts who are kept on a strict diet of some attention and occasional hugs. The frequently touched children learn to walk and talk sooner. They tend to be more independent, more assertive, and more confident of themselves. In short, they tend to thrive.

What I was observing as I watched the two girls playing in the yard was the result of basic parenting beliefs and styles being acted out in the personalities of the children. Michelle was active, interested, and self-confident. Marlena appeared passive, detached, and not nearly so sure of herself.

It isn't that one parent was good and the other bad, that one loved her child more than the other, or anything like that. The issue is that the effect of one parenting style on the behavior of the child was more desirable than the other. It was more effective.

At one point while I was watching the girls, Michelle went over to her mother and crawled into her lap to be held. After a moment of watching them cuddle happily, Marlena's mother got up from her chair, went to her child, and sat down beside her. She talked and played with Marlena for a few minutes, and then she picked up her daughter and pulled her into her lap with a long hug. Now I was amazed for another reason. Marlena began to chatter and wave her arms as Michelle had been doing earlier. It was as though the child had come alive! Like a plant being watered and fed, nurtured and cared for in the warmth of the sun's life-giving light, Marlena seemed to blossom before my very eyes. It was at that moment that I came to appreciate just what a difference a hug makes!

Intimacy is a basic need of all human life and is most often experienced through touching.

Our Need to Be Touched

Intimacy is a basic need of all human life. It's a powerful, driving force in the lives of those who don't have it and a sustaining force in the lives of those who do. It's the strength of every healthy family or the weakness of those who seek it beyond the limits of commitment and compassion. It's the hope and promise of every love or the despair and sorrow of lonely people who have sought it but not found it. Life without intimacy is a life adrift, uncommitted, leaving untapped the deepest feelings of caring and sharing, those emotions that not only bring vitality to life but provide much of its meaning and purpose as well. People need people. Even more, people need special people to make them feel special. Special people are those whom we dare to reach out and touch and those we allow to touch us. It is with these others that we share ourselves in intimate relationships.

Adults as well as children need to be touched and held occasionally, to feel safe and secure in the warmth of another's arms, to trust enough to share one's deepest hopes and dreams while vulnerable enough to expose one's deepest hurts and disappointments. It is out of such intimacy that bonding occurs, and bonding is the key to commitment in any relationship. It is also an important part of emotional health.

Studies of infants raised in institutions with a minimum of physical contact have clearly demonstrated that babies need more than food, shelter, and clothing. They also need physical and emotional stimulation, tender touches, affectionate cud-dling, warm smiles, eager encouragement, and other forms of intimacy if they're to develop normally and thrive. Without it, children may suffer severe developmental delays that may result in learning disabilities, failure to learn to walk or talk, social and emotional problems, and general failure to thrive. Some may become passive, withdrawn, and unresponsive to the world in which they live, as though life holds no interest for them. Others may simply wither and die.

Although it's possible to be emotionally intimate without physically touching, as in the case of friends praying together or two people in a counseling relationship, intimacy is most often expressed and experienced through touching another person and allowing oneself to be touched. It involves physical contact of some sort, be it a handshake, a pat on the back, a hug, a kiss, or a caress.

Touching another person, whether adult or child, is done for a reason. People generally don't touch the body of another person without some purpose in mind. Most touches are done for right and proper reasons, as expressions of love and caring perhaps. But this is not the only reason people touch each other. There are others. Sometimes people touch in an attempt to inflict pain or to use, exploit, manipulate, or even control another person.

---

*Some touches are bad and
ought to be avoided.
Touch should never be used
to exploit or manipulate.*

Good Touching and Bad Touching

Good touches are those that make the recipient feel good about who and what he is as a person. Hugging a child, for ex-ample, tells the child not only that he's loved, but also that he's worthy of the time, effort, and attention of the parent. It assures him that he's wanted and accepted, that nothing is wrong with him. It teaches him he's good enough to win parental approval. Children who *think* they're good are likely to *feel* good about themselves, and their behavior is sure to reflect that feeling.

Good touches also make the child feel good about the parent. They stir up warm feelings that inevitably will be expressed. A warm smile most often will bring a warm smile in return. The best way to get a hug is to give one.

Good touches also make the child feel good about the relationship. Most important of all, they teach the child that the relationship can be trusted to supply essential needs and provide opportunities to have wants and wishes fulfilled. It's a relationship that will not change day by day, that can be trusted to be there even when the going gets tough. It's a relationship that is permanent and can never be lost or taken away.

Bad touching, on the other hand, has just the opposite effect. It makes the child feel bad about himself—unwanted, unlovable, unworthy, or inadequate. The child may come to perceive himself as a mistake that should never have happened. Children who *think* they're bad are likely to *feel* bad about themselves. And again, behavior is sure to reflect that feeling.

Bad touching also makes the child feel bad about the parent. When parents hurt them, children most often defend themselves by blaming themselves. This is because a child psychologically needs to believe his parents are "good" all the time and never make mistakes. To him, his parents are everything, the whole world, the only reality and truth he knows. He needs desperately to believe he lives in a good and benevolent world. Otherwise, there's no hope. If the child thinks he's the one who's bad, he can also think, *I'll change. I'll become good and what they want me to be, and then they'll love me and take care of me.*

Bad touching makes the child feel bad about the relationship as well. More important than anything else, bad touching teaches a child that his parents can't be trusted to provide the care and nurture he so desperately needs. He learns he must take care of himself because he can no longer afford the risk of

60

respecting parental authority and allowing himself to be dependent on their good will and intentions.

He knows the relationship not only will change, but must change. It can't be trusted from moment to moment to be the same as it was just yesterday. And children learn this lesson at a surprisingly early age.

Distinguishing Good from Bad Touches

There is an infinite number of possible touches from an equal number of possible sources when children interact with other people. Except in clear cases of physical abuse, it's sometimes difficult for parents to know how to distinguish harmful touches from those that enrich the life of their child. Perhaps the following method will help you in this regard.

Consider the touch in question. Then ask yourself the following six questions about the touch and determine how many of the six criteria of good touching apply to the touch you are considering.

1. *Who is doing the touching?* Good touches, those that result in the greatest benefit for the child, come most often from a parent, guardian, or close family member. Touches by other people may be acceptable, but they fall into the category of okay touches rather than good touches.

2. *What kind of touch is it?* Good touches are nonviolent and don't inflict physical pain or emotional discomfort on the child.

3. *Why is the child being touched?* Good touches are expressions of love and caring that are offered to meet the needs of the child, to comfort and help the child.

4. *When is the child being touched?* Good touches occur at appropriate times and in appropriate settings. Generally, appropriate times and settings are those that enhance the child's feelings of self-esteem, achievement, and well-being.

5. *What is the age of the child?* Good and bad touches may change with the age of the child. For example, bathing a child of three years would certainly be considered good touching. How-

ever, the same kind of touching when the child is thirteen years old becomes an entirely different matter. Good touches are those appropriate for the child's age and development.

6. *What is the effect of the touch on the child?* Good touches enhance rather than diminish a child's health and welfare; they build a child up rather than tear him down; they feel good to the child rather than bad; they don't result in physical or mental discomfort in the child nor cause emotional conflict or distress.

How many of the six criteria of good touching did the touch you are considering meet? Good touches, those most desirable and most beneficial to the child, will meet all six. Use the scale below to rate the touch.

Met all 6	good touch
Met only 5	okay touch
Met only 4	questionable touch
Met only 3	suspicious touch
Met only 2	not okay touch
Met only 1	bad touch

As a rule, all touches except those that rate as good or okay should be avoided. More questionable touches will undoubtedly have at least some negative impact upon the physical or emotional health of the child. Let's look at a couple of examples to clarify how parents can use this rating method as a tool for avoiding bad touches with their children and to improve their overall parenting.

Twelve-year-old Joan is at the wedding of her brother. During the reception, Uncle Charlie invites her to dance. Having met Uncle Charlie only once before, Joan is reluctant but finally gives in to his request. While they are dancing, Uncle Charlie allows his hand to slip well below the belt line on her back. Joan is uncomfortable and doesn't know what to do. She's relieved when the music finally stops and the dance is over. Is Uncle Charlie's misplaced hand a good touch or a bad touch?

Few people would argue that this is at the very least an inappropriate touch. There might be some difference of opinion, however, on whether it would fall into the category of a suspicious touch, a not okay touch, or a bad touch. Let's classify it using the method described.

Who is doing the touching? Uncle Charlie, a remote family member whom Joan doesn't know well.

What kind of touch is it? Though not physically painful, it's emotionally uncomfortable.

Why is she being touched? We can't know the intentions of Uncle Charlie. However, given the nature of the touch and where it's located on the body, we can reasonably assume that the purpose of the touch is not to express love and caring, but is designed to meet Uncle Charlie's needs in some way.

When is she being touched? Clearly, there is no appropriate time or place for a touch that has sexual overtones.

What is the age of the child? Joan is twelve years old, far too young for this kind of touching.

What is the effect of the touch on Joan? Joan is confused and uncomfortable, and she experiences internal conflict and distress because of the touch.

Obviously, Uncle Charlie's touching meets none of the criteria of good touching. Therefore, it falls into the category of a bad touch on the scale, a touch that should be avoided.

Let's consider another example. Eight-year-old Sharon has been having trouble learning to subtract numbers in math. Finally, after days of effort, she gets a perfect score on a test involving subtraction. Knowing how hard Sharon has worked, the teacher is pleased and wants Sharon to know it. As Sharon comes up to retrieve her test paper, the teacher puts her arm around her shoulders and tells her in front of the class how proud she is of her. This sounds like a good touch. Let's see how it rates on the scale.

Who is doing the touching? A teacher, not a guardian or a close family member.

What kind of touch is it? It's nonviolent and inflicts no pain, and Sharon experiences no emotional discomfort.

Why is the child being touched? As an expression of caring and pride in the child's accomplishment, we may assume.

When is the child being touched? The touch is occurring in public, in front of the class, and most likely will enhance Sharon's self-esteem.

What is the age of the child? Sharon is eight years old. This kind of touching is appropriate for all ages.

What is the effect of the touch on the child? The touch makes Sharon feel good about herself, her relationship with the teacher, and what she has accomplished.

In this situation, the touch rates a 5 on the good touching scale. This places it in the category of an okay touch.

All children need lots and lots of good touching. But no child needs abusive touching or touching that leaves him hurt or damaged. Good and okay touching should be sought, provided, and encouraged at every opportunity. Questionable and suspicious touches should raise some concern in the minds of the parents and should be avoided if possible. Bad touching and not okay touching should raise a great deal of parental concern. They should be prevented when they have not yet occurred and stopped when they are occurring, and necessary steps should be taken to make sure they don't happen again. It's the bad and not okay touches that pose the greatest threat to the physical and emotional health of our children. We must act quickly and decisively with these forms of touching to protect our children.

Touching That Hurts

Some kinds of touching are always bad in all situations due to their nature and the sure effect upon the child. These touches are clearly abusive, a threat to the health and development of the child.

Double-message Touching

Every touch is also a form of communication. It carries a message. Sometimes the message is clear, as with a slap across the face. Other touching messages may be vague and unclear, as might be the case with a touch on the shoulder.

What a Difference a Hug Makes!

What is most confusing to a child and so results in the greatest emotional conflict is when the child receives two messages simultaneously from the parent, a verbal message telling him one thing and a touching message telling him something entirely different, perhaps even contradictory. Consider the possible effect on four-year-old Jason as he attempts to show the picture he has just colored to his mother. She's sitting at the table in the dining room, writing letters. Jason enters the room calling out eagerly to his mother while holding the prize out for her to see. Mother is irritated by the intrusion into her thoughts. Glancing briefly at the picture, she turns Jason around and gives him a little shove back in the direction from which he has come with the words, "What a nice picture, Jason. Thank you for showing it to me. Can you go back and color Mama another one?"

The message to Jason is clearly a double one. On the one hand, he hears his mother telling him what he's done is good and she's pleased. But her touching message is quite different. She turns the child away as though she really doesn't care about what he's done or why. The dilemma for Jason, as for all children in similar situations, is which of the two messages is he to believe?

Children tend to measure the value and worth of their efforts by the parental response they bring. Those efforts that bring a great deal of attention and praise will be valued more than those that bring little. In this case, it's likely that Jason's initial excitement and pleasure over the picture he has colored will fade quickly in light of his mother's response to it. Instead of providing him a source of personal pride and achievement, a gift of himself to his mother, the picture is now likely to find its way into a garbage can, unwanted, inadequate, and worthless. On the other hand, the verbal message may encourage him to try again, and try even harder, to win his mother's approval. Repeated failures to do so, however, can result in his feeling so inadequate as an artist that he will no longer make any effort to meet those assignments in school that require coloring. This is a form of learned disability.

Inconsistent Touching

Like most other interaction with children, in order for touching to have maximum emotional benefit to the developing child, it must be consistent. What would be the emotional effect on your child if at one time you picked him up and offered a hug and comfort following a fall, and then after the next fall you pushed him away? Surely he would be confused, not knowing for certain whether you were a trusted source of comfort or a source of rejection to be avoided. Certain parental reactions must be so certain for the child that they are utterly predictable; this provides essential peace and security.

It's often fear of the unknown, not knowing what's likely to happen next, that fuels emotional distress. Out of such uncertainty grow tentative children, inhibited and afraid to try for fear of what might happen if they did try and then failed.

If your child's bedtime is to be accompanied by a good-night hug from you, it's important that you make sure no other kind of touching takes its place. Bedtime and warm hugging must become synonymous, predictable, and sure things for your child regardless of what has occurred during the day. Therein is its greatest emotional benefit.

The Untouched Child

Just as bad touching can seriously threaten the health and development of children, not touching them at all can be an equally serious threat to their welfare. All human beings, regardless of age, need to feel the warmth of another's touch on their skin, to experience the life-sustaining pulse of someone else's heart pressed close to their own, to feel the rhythmic breathing that is life, and to know the smells that are human. Studies have shown the importance of close physical contact between the newborn infant and parents during the early hours and days of life in order for maximum, healthy bonding to occur.

Without such intimate and frequent contact, it's unlikely that a child will develop normally, nor will he thrive. For the seriously deprived, their young lives will take shape as they evolve around the emptiness, the void, the physical barrier that exists between themselves and other people. They're likely to grow up believing they're unlovable, certainly untouchable. This single belief may have a fatal effect on every relationship the individual may attempt as an adult, leaving the person trapped in the prison of his own body, alone, with little or no hope for intimacy.

It's important that conscientious parents give their children lots and lots of good touches: rocking, holding, hugging, and caressing. But it's equally important that these touches make the child feel good, not bad, that they enhance the child's self-esteem rather than diminish it. Warm, affectionate hugs by parents make children feel loved, accepted, and secure in the relationship and in their world. Secure children are free to experience childhood fully, to explore its every magical possibility, and to build a foundation for adulthood that is not only healthy but also an endless reservoir of hope.

Points to Remember

There's a distinct difference between good touches and bad touches. Good touches make children feel good about themselves, the relationship, and what's happening. Bad touches exploit children for the gratification of an adult.

1. Using the scale provided, rate touches in terms of being good, okay, questionable, suspicious, not okay, and bad. Keep in mind that all touches should be avoided except those that rate as good or okay.

2. Avoid double-message touches that give the child opposite, different, or conflicting messages.

3. Keep touches consistent, a predictable part of certain kinds of parent-child interaction, such as hugs at bedtime.

Chapter 4
At the Sound of the Whistle!

Do you remember how Maria was introduced to the children in the movie *The Sound of Music?* The children's father, Baron von Trapp, was a retired naval officer, raising the children alone after his wife died. Standing with Maria in the expansive foyer of that beautiful home, the baron pulled a bosun mate's whistle from his pocket and piped a message to the children. Almost instantaneously the children appeared from every corner of the house, each dressed neatly in a starched and ironed uniform. Together they marched in single file down the stairs to form an inspection line in front of Maria and their father. Still at attention, the children introduced themselves by stepping forward in order and then reclaiming their place in line. Maria was as astonished by the children's performance as their father was pleased. It was clear to all of us that the baron directed his family with the same military command he did his naval ships. There was no doubt who ran that family! The baron was in total control.

Few of us would argue that these children were well-disciplined, controlled by the iron will of their father. Yet, as later scenes in the movie clearly showed, the children were also absolutely miserable, living in a military camp rather than a home. Since their mother's death, their father had fulfilled his duties as a single parent by assuming total control of the children and their lives. But in gaining that control, the baron and his children lost something—something vital and important to all families. They lost the physical and emotional intimacy that is the life and warmth of any healthy relationship. There's little room for feelings in a family where order and control are *the* primary concerns. The baron and his children were estranged in their relationship. They were foreign to one another, alienated and lonely. Yet, the viewer could hardly doubt they all loved each other.

Then into this wasteland of human emotions stepped Maria, a wellspring of bubbling life, love, and music. And what a difference she made! The warmth of her love melted their frozen hearts. The freedom of her living and the joy it brought them all unlocked the prison of their own lives. Even the baron began to understand that people are more important than the rules used to control them.

Parents: Masters or Servants of Children?

There are as many styles of raising children as there are parents to raise them. No particular style is all right or all wrong all the time and in every situation. There are advantages to each, as well as disadvantages. But of all the parenting styles imaginable, two that are opposite extremes stand out as most harmful to the emotional health and development of children—and both can be practiced by parents with the best intentions but who don't understand the consequences of what they're doing. One is the style of domination. Dominating parents dictate their children's lives, maintaining absolute control at all times, like Baron von Trapp. These parents function as masters over their children, controlling and supervising their children's steps along the straight and narrow path.

The other potentially harmful style of parenting is servanthood. These parents exercise no control over their children. They're inclined to give their children everything they want, but little of what they need most beyond the basic necessities of life. These parents become servants to their children, tending to their every desire. Such parents have, for all practical purposes, abdicated their roles as parents. They have essentially abandoned their children to grow up as best they can without guidance, limits, or controls.

Two styles of parenting are more damaging emotionally to children than any others: the styles of domination and servanthood.

Children raised in families where there is too much or not enough parental control have a higher risk of developing emotional problems in adulthood than children raised in families where a healthy balance exists. As always, it's the extremes of too much or not enough control that seem to cause the most problems. Robotic children and untamed children rarely grow into well-adjusted adults.

Turn Loose! I Can't Breathe!

Andy was truly an outstanding child. He seemed to excel at just about everything he tried. By the age of ten he was a straight *A* student and a standout on his athletic teams. His parents were very proud of him, and Andy seemed proud of himself.

Then came the letter from the school psychologist. The school wanted to test him to determine if he was a certified gifted child. Both parents were excited that their son might qualify for the special academic program offered gifted children in their school district. Their imaginations began to soar as a whole new realm of possibilities opened up for Andy in their minds. They were clearly more nervous about the test than was Andy.

The tests results came back positive. Andy was indeed a gifted child. He enrolled in the gifted program at another school at the start of the next academic year.

That was a year ago. When his parents brought him to me, Andy was eleven years old and in the sixth grade. His parents were worried about him. They had tried everything they could think of to help him, but nothing seemed to work. Andy's grades had fallen from straight *A*'s to *C*'s and *D*'s. He also seemed to have lost all interest in athletics. His performance on the field during games was mediocre at best. He spent most of his free time either reading alone in his room or watching television. His parents were desperate. They didn't know what was wrong with the child, much less what to do about it.

It didn't take long for us to discover that the changes in Andy's attitudes and behaviors began shortly after he was certified by the school psychologist as a gifted child. But as we talked over the next several weeks, we came to see that it was not Andy who had begun to change but his parents.

What changed first was his parents' perception of him. Instead of being a normal child who worked hard to excel at school and in athletics, Andy became an exceptional child in their minds. He wasn't like other children and couldn't be treated like other children. He needed to be challenged, to be directed and pushed to reach his full potential.

As their perception of Andy changed, so did their attitude toward him. They became more demanding of him, expecting more and settling for less. Second or third place was no longer good enough. He had to finish first in everything, to be the best. If he didn't, it could only be because he wasn't trying hard enough or they were failing as parents.

As their attitude toward Andy changed, so did their behavior. No longer was he treated like a child. No longer was he allowed to be carefree and irresponsible in a normal childhood. From his parents' perspective, Andy went into training. Special attention was given to every area of his life. His diet was changed to reflect only the most nutritious foods—no more snack foods or desserts. His day-to-day life was placed on a rigid schedule that dictated his every activity from the time he got up in the morning to the time lights went out at night. He became his parents' preoccupation. It was as though he was their pet project! Most of their free time was spent with their attention focused on him. They wanted to make sure he had every opportunity to develop his potential fully.

Andy's attitude and behavior began to change in response to the increasing demands of his parents. They were treating him differently, but he had a hard time understanding why. He didn't feel different, look different, or even think differently. But something was different. It frightened him to see such changes in his parents. He was never quite sure what they wanted from him. Unsure of himself and apprehensive about his parents' reactions, Andy began to concentrate less and less on his schoolwork and sports and more and more on his parents and the changes that now separated them. As he did, his grades began to slip, along with his performance on the field. His parents' reaction was to push him harder, to make even more demands of him.

By the time Andy came to see me, all the fun and joy in life was gone for him. Life was a job. He was no longer proud of himself. He knew that his parents were disappointed in him. He had somehow let them down. That hurt, so much so that he became depressed and withdrew more and more into himself for protection from his parents' expectations and his own desperate feelings. The more Andy failed to live up to their expectations, the more his parents tried to control his every move. They even came to perceive his inability to perform up to their elevated standards as simple rebelliousness and a desire on his part to embarrass them publicly. Many times in anger and frustration they punished Andy. Sometimes harshly. The effect on him was to cause him to withdraw even more.

The family became caught up in a vicious circle out of which there seemed to be no escape. They were all trapped.

Watching Andy sitting passively on the couch across from me, I was reminded of someone strangling to death. It was as though he couldn't get enough breath, as if he was suffocating.

In their eagerness to be outstanding parents for their outstanding child, Andy's parents had overreacted and had literally taken charge of Andy, his life, and his future. In their desire to make Andy into everything he could be, they lost him.

Dominating parents usually possess certain characteristics that distinguish them from other parents. And while your family situation may not be as extreme as Andy's, look at these traits in terms of whether you as a parent have any tendencies in this direction. As mentioned earlier, even the best moms and dads can slip into harmful parenting styles without realizing it.

First, dominating parents believe the most important function of parenting is to control the thinking and behavior of their children. They believe their success as parents will be measured only in terms of how well their children behave. They confuse discipline and control. Even worse, they perceive the role of a parent more in terms of a rule enforcer than as a teacher and a guide.

Second, dominating parents tend to believe there exists no higher power, no greater authority in the family than their own wills. They rule the family with an iron hand. Their word is law, and they have the power and right to enforce it by whatever means they deem necessary. Yet, they are above the law. These are parents who tend to parent using a "Do as I say, not as I do" approach.

Third, there is no greater crime in such families than disobedience. Because it threatens parental authority within the family, disobedience must be quickly and harshly punished. Compliance and submission to the wills of the parents are valued over all else in the family. Oftentimes, love and parental acceptance are contingent upon the children's degree of obedience.

Fourth, dominating parents tend to demand a great deal from their children. Often their expectations are unrealistic and beyond the capacity of the children to meet. They usually have poor knowledge of child development and what can be reasonably expected at each developmental age. The result is that failure to meet parental expectations is often seen as willful disobedience and is punished.

Fifth, these parents generally have rules for everything. Even simple tasks have hard and fast procedures that must be followed. There is a right way and a wrong way of doing everything because all aspects of human living fall into a clear category of either right or wrong. There are few gray areas of ambiguity or uncertainty. The good child is obedient and rewarded. The bad child is disobedient and punished. In such families, there is a tendency for the rules to become more important than the lives they control.

Sixth, the parents tend to view mistakes as crimes. All children make mistakes. Making mistakes is as much a part of learning as is repetition, and little learning occurs without them. For example, sometimes it's helpful to learn what *is* by first learning what is *not*. Learning how to succeed is often learned through many failures. However, many dominating parents misunderstand normal, predictable, and healthy childhood mistakes as willful acts of disobedience with malicious intent, as crimes deserving punishment. The punishment used by these parents is often harsh and extreme by most standards, but they see it as just and fair considering the seriousness of the crime.

Seventh, they control through fear. The primary feature of dominating parents is that they tend to be authoritarian. They tolerate no opposition and rely heavily on physical and emotional punishment to ensure compliance and submission to their wills. Such a style of parenting inspires fear.

During the first year or so of life, you must do everything for your baby. The child is totally dependent upon you for all things. At this point in the child's life, parents who don't assume full control of his life may do him great harm. But as the child grows and matures, he learns more and more to do things for himself. He gains a sense of independence from his parents. The task of parents then is to gradually loosen and release control in most areas affecting the child's life. In extreme cases, however, dominating parents have difficulty surrendering that control. To do so, they must trust the child's capability and willingness to manage aspects of his own life.

Most domineering people are insecure, afraid of rejection and failure. Immersed as they are in fears of failure, human weakness, and the negative possibilities that exist in all things, they often maintain unrealistically high expectations of their children—perhaps as a way of overcoming the failures they see all around them. By demanding excellence in all areas all the time, these parents literally set their children up to fail.

Children who continually fail in the eyes of their parents, who never can seem to be good enough, smart enough, fast enough, or tough enough to win the acceptance and approval of their parents, carry a great burden of guilt and personal shame. Most children want desperately to be what their parents want them to be. Those who can't, in time, will quit trying to please their parents altogether and just give up, resigning themselves to a fate they come to see as unavoidable. These children will learn quickly that it's less painful to cope with their parents' rejection than with their constant disappointment. This is a dynamic common to many children of domineering parents. It's called survival through assumed disability.

These children learn early in life that they "can't." Children who can't are children who "won't." They won't even try. They assume the role of perpetual victim.

Children who "can't" usually turn out to be children who "won't." Believing themselves inadequate, they won't even try.

But Don't You Even Care?

At one point in my life, I worked in a small elementary school as a teacher's assistant while continuing my own education.

There was one child who attended that school whom I will never forget. His name was Shean.

Shean came from a large family. There were six children, and he was the oldest. Both his parents worked during the day and were often late returning home in the evenings. It was obvious to any observer that they loved their children and worked hard to provide them the material things important to every childhood.

Shean was always well dressed and seemed physically healthy. He had a ready smile whenever any adult would pause long enough to look at him. But there were times I would watch him in class or on the playground when he was not aware of me. It was during those times that I saw clearly the loneliness that was so much a part of his life.

Being the oldest, Shean was pretty much expected by his parents to take care of himself. Most of their time and energy after work and on weekends were taken up by the younger children. As a result, even at the age of nine, Shean spent very little time at home. He would eat there, sleep there at night, and go there during harsh weather. But most of the time, when he was not in school he was on the street.

One day Shean asked me to give him a ride downtown after school. He was going to a movie, he told me. He had asked his parents for the money that morning before leaving for school. Without a thought, or asking him why he wanted it, they gave it to him. They gave him just about everything he asked for.

I was surprised at his request, but I assured him of the ride if his parents agreed. I stressed that we would have to get their permission first. It was then he made the statement that has haunted me ever since: "I can do what I want to. They don't care!"

They don't care. A simple statement that says so much. I have wondered many times since then whether Shean really believed that or not. Did they not care about his catching a ride downtown to see a movie, or did they not care about him?

Even though his parents thought they were doing everything they could to take good care of him, I suspect Shean believed they didn't care about him. Because they paid so little attention to him and allowed him to do as he pleased, Shean felt unimportant in their lives, as though what happened to him really didn't matter. He could see the active roles played by other parents in the lives of their children. He could see they cared because they were there. But he was alone.

Shean's parents served him like servants. They tried to meet his every want, but rarely was there any thought of what he might need. Rarely did they impose any limits or controls upon him. Because of the lack of some controls, Shean was a child at great risk of serious problems.

Parents who function as servants to their children also usually possess certain characteristics that distinguish them from other parents. Once again, as you read these, examine your own parenting style for any tendencies in this direction.

First, these parents believe good parents are perfect parents. Being a perfect parent means never making a mistake or experiencing anything but positive thoughts and feelings about their children. Such a notion is an illusion. There's no such thing as a perfect parent. Nor is such a creature possible! But servant parents try to be perfect by subjecting their own wills to those of their children. By avoiding conflict and confrontation, they avoid those unpleasant—though natural—feelings that make them feel inadequate as parents. Or the fear of failure is so great that they make no effort to be strong parents at all.

Second, they believe their children always come first. This belief is certainly necessary for the survival of children during those first couple of years during which they're totally helpless and must rely on their parents for all things. But as children mature and become more independent, these parents continue to live their lives around the wants and needs of their children. They can literally become slaves to the whims of children.

Third, they believe parenting comes naturally. It's instinctual, they think, an inherited ability derived from ancestors. These parents rely on their own judgment in all matters. They see no value in education or discussion of similar situations with other parents of children the same age. They believe their good intentions will bring about the desired good result. Most of these parents are unaware of how much of their thinking and feeling about their children is motivated by their own sense of guilt or inadequacy rather than by what is in their children's best interests.

Effective parenting involves more than good intentions. It involves preparation and ongoing support.

Fourth, these parents have high hopes. Unlike their counterparts who expect too much of their children and seem constantly disappointed, servant parents tend to expect very little of their children and are rarely pleasantly surprised. They expect little, but have high hopes. Their hope is that their children will grow normally and develop into the kind of people they desire—that everything will turn out for the best in the end.

Fifth, they believe good parents have happy children. Servant parents tend to look for happiness in their children as witness to their parenting success. In their minds, happy children are usually those who get the best of whatever they want. Satisfied children are happy children. These parents live to please. Their reward is an occasional smile. They understand happiness to be the absence of want. Rarely do they consider happiness in children as being the result of feelings: feeling loved, wanted, and secure in their world.

Finally, they fear rejection. Most servant parents fear their children will turn against them should they be too firm or expect too much. They tend to be insecure people, lacking in self-esteem, and unsure in relationships. Unsure of their children's love, they dare not do anything that might threaten the relationship. In living to please their children, they live in hopes of earning their love. Such parents are slaves to their own insecurities.

The Right Fit

It's essential for the health and welfare of your children and your family that you as a parent maintain control. You must set reasonable limits and reasonably enforce them. You must provide the material and social needs of your family as well as protect it from all harm—either from within or without. It's important that you maintain order and structure for the benefit of all.

The difficulty for most parents, however, is in knowing what to control and what not to control. Recognizing what is a real threat to the health and welfare of the family or its members can be a challenge for any parent.

Many parents become confused and insecure at this point, believing that all their responses must be firm and that it's better to err on the side of too much control. How often have we heard others tell us, "Be firm!" when it comes to our children? That sounds nice, but it's impossible always and in every situation to be firm. We aren't robots who can be programmed to react the same way always. Nor is it desirable for parents always to be firm.

Keeping in mind that the goal of effective parenting is to teach children to control themselves, you can use the following guidelines to overcome some of your confusion in this area of parental control.

Every human relationship, particularly the one that exists between you and your child, has three basic categories of acceptable and unacceptable behaviors. For the sake of clarity, I call them the No Behaviors, the Maybe Behaviors, and the Yes Behaviors. Each type of behavior is designed to accomplish a specific goal and requires a different level of parental control. Let's see how they compare.

Category One: No Behaviors consist of what are called nonnegotiable behaviors in any relationship. These are acts or behaviors that will not be tolerated under any circumstance. The nonnegotiables reflect what is considered essential for protecting, preserving, and maintaining the relationship. They represent the *minimal standards of conduct* that must be respected and enforced in order to maintain a viable relationship. In a family relationship, nonnegotiables might be biting, kicking, or hitting—all acts of violence that could threaten the welfare of the family and its members.

It's in this area of interaction that children learn limits. For the health and welfare of all, these nonnegotiables must be enforced. Every attempt by the child to exhibit nonnegotiable behavior must be met by a firm, consistent, determined, and nonnegotiable response on the part of the parent. Nonnegotiables *should never be compromised* because they're the foundation upon which personalities, families, and societies are built. They're the pillars of human conduct, the framework of every relationship.

Category Two: Maybe Behaviors consist of what are called negotiable behaviors in any relationship. Negotiable behaviors include that wide range of activities important to the health and welfare of children and families, but not so vital as to threaten their existence should they be altered. They represent the *accepted standards of conduct* that are acknowledged as important, have some flexibility, and for which an occasional exception exists. Negotiables in a family might be bedtime, when chores are done, who folds the clothes or washes the dishes, what time dinner is served, when friends can be in the house, and so forth.

It's in this area of interaction that children learn assertiveness and decision-making skills. These behaviors provide excellent opportunities to teach children priority setting, considering alternatives, making choices, living with the consequences of those choices, and determining what's important to them. This is a wonderful opportunity to teach your children how to negotiate for what they want rather than fight or manipulate for it.

Category Three: Yes Behaviors are those that almost always are an issue of free will or personal choice. These are behaviors of no concern to anyone but the child and pose no threat or challenge to the authority of the parent or to the welfare of the family. Generally, free-will behaviors relate to issues of personal taste, personal preference, and personal likes. No harm will come to the child or family if the child chooses to drink out of the red cup with the dog on it rather than the yellow one offered him, wears brown socks instead of blue, or prefers to eat his meal one item at a time rather than all together.

It's in this area of interaction that children learn self-expression. These behaviors are opportunities to experience one's uniqueness, to celebrate differences by not being like everyone else in the family. They provide excellent opportunities for building a positive self-image and self-esteem in the child, both of which are essential for emotional health. They allow the child to develop unique talents and abilities; they encourage the expression of tastes and preferences without interference or control by parents. Free-will behaviors are harmless to others but of tremendous benefit to the child.

In the category of nonnegotiable behaviors, parents should exercise total control with immovable resistance. Your response should be consistently no.

In the category of negotiable behaviors, parents should exercise some control and some resistance. Your response should be consistently maybe.

In the category of personal choice, parents should exercise no control and no resistance. Your response should be consistently yes.

But what is ultimately most important to the emotional health and development of your children is that you be as consistent in your responses as possible. The relationship becomes predictable and manageable for them as they feel more and more secure in their trust of it and you. With a growing sense of trust and security will come a growing respect for your authority and the limits you impose upon them. These are the essentials of a healthy parent-child relationship.

Points to Remember

Adults are and must always remain the authority figures within the family. Only they have the wisdom and experience necessary for managing the family and the lives of its members. But all parents need to remember that the primary goal of parenting is not to control the thinking and behavior of children at all costs. The goal is to teach children to control their own thinking and behavior. This is called discipline and is quite different from punishment.

1. Although parents do, in fact, control the power within the family, it's important that children be allowed to participate in decision making, particularly in areas that concern them directly.

2. Obedience that is demanded is likely to be resented and is the fuel of rebellion.

3. Adults' expectations of children should be appropriate and reasonable for their level of development and age.

4. Children aren't little adults. They're children with children's minds and bodies and spirits. They can't be expected to function as adults.

5. The spirit of the law is as important as the letter. Laws within the family are important as long as they enhance the health and welfare of its members.

6. Children don't commit crimes; they make mistakes. Mistakes provide parents with excellent opportunities for teaching.

7. Controlling children through fear and intimidation is doomed to failure, for inevitably the day will come when there will be a power shift in the relationship and it will be they who have the power to control with fear and intimidation.

8. Discipline and punishment aren't the same thing, nor is their effect upon children the same.

Chapter 5
It Hurts Me More Than It Hurts You!

In my first book, *Cry Out!* (Abingdon Press, 1984), in which I identified myself as "Peter," I described what happened to my mother after she and my father were divorced and the effect it had on me as a child.

> No more walks in the park or drives in the country, no more hugs or bedtime stories, and no more chocolate milkshakes. Nothing was the same. Even his mother had changed. She would often sleep most of the day or watch television for long hours at a time. Sometimes Peter would find her crying into the pillow on the bed. He worried that she did not laugh and play with them much any more. She always seemed so tired. Sitting close beside her on the couch he could feel the sadness and quiet desperation out of which she now lived (p. 23).

My mother was depressed at the breakup of her marriage. And rightly so. She was suffering. Her family had been torn apart. She desperately needed some help and support.

Many suffering parents become so involved in their own problems during times of great stress and turmoil that they don't see the effect their trials are having on the children in the family. Just witnessing the suffering of my mother was incredibly frightening and disturbing to me. It hurts to have to watch helplessly while someone you love hurts.

Children often experience deep emotional reactions to the suffering of their parents. Whether they understand intellectually or not, children know that their personal welfare depends on the health and welfare of their parents. Children tend to experience their vulnerabilities acutely during times when one or both parents are sick or hurt. When parents are out of control, children tend to lose control as well.

Watching his parents suffer heightens a child's sense of vulnerability and involves him in the suffering as well. A child trying to cope with a parent out of control is likely to lose control as well.

It's not so much that you, as a parent, have problems that can be potentially harmful to your children. All parents have problems. The greatest impact on your children comes from how you go about resolving your problems—or whether you try to solve them at all. My mother made no effort that I was aware of to get help for herself until it was too late. Making no attempt to help yourself can instill a sense of hopelessness about life in children.

Just as seriously, children often share the symptoms of suffering they see in their parents. Consider what your children do when they see you laughing. What happens to them when you cry? When you get angry with someone outside the family? Children tend to share our adult feelings as though they were their own. Now imagine what happens to your children when you are seriously and chronically depressed, suffer from chronic anxiety, or have a drinking problem. Because of their limited understanding, children can even suffer more from adult problems than from their own.

The Effects of Suffering

People hurt. Not only do they hurt themselves, but they also hurt each other. Sometimes it's by accident, sometimes on purpose. Sometimes the hurt comes from something within them or around them over which they have no control. But every day, and in every way imaginable, people everywhere experience pain of some kind. Whether it's physical pain caused by hunger, a hangnail, or a twisted ankle, or emotional pain caused by rejection, betrayal, or personal loss, coping with pain and discomfort is as much a part of successful living as is breathing. There's no life free of it. Indeed, life could not exist without it. Pain is as necessary for maintaining life as avoiding pain is necessary for preserving life. It works as an early warning signal alerting the mind to hazards threatening the health and wellbeing of the body. It's a clear message that something is wrong and needs immediate attention. It brings help when help is needed most. Yet, too much pain for too long resulting from severe trauma can be deadly.

It's one thing to experience pain and quite another to suffer from it. Most people experience brief physical and emotional discomfort when the needle punctures the skin during a vaccination, but few of us actually suffer because of it. The fleeting pain caused by getting a shot falls well within the range of the coping capabilities of most people. We can handle it without great effort, and within seconds it's all over.

Suffering occurs when the pain or discomfort is severe and prolonged and there's no immediate relief available. Suffering generally occurs in those vital areas of greatest concern for us: our lives, our relationships with loved ones, and our careers. It's in these important areas that a little discomfort can result in a lot of distress. For it's here that we're most vulnerable. The distress caused by an argument with a fellow employee can be mild compared to the distress we may feel after a fight with a spouse. Certainly, the distress of losing a car is nothing when compared to that caused by the loss of a child.

Severe and prolonged discomfort forces us beyond our normal, comfortable, everyday methods of coping. When ordinary methods don't work, extraordinary methods must be found and utilized. Such demands for adjustment can stimulate additional suffering. They can force us to put other concerns aside and turn inward, away from the world and those around us, to focus our attention and energy on the need to cope. How much suffering will result depends primarily on how radical and how many adjustments have to be made in order to cope. A tension headache, for example, which can be relieved with aspirin and a few minutes of relaxation, will cause little suffering. A migraine headache, on the other hand, may result in a great deal of suffering because of the severity of the pain, because relief is not immediately available, and because it forces us to put our personal well-being above all other concerns. Suffering tends to force us out of daily routines. It interrupts and interferes with normal, daily functioning.

Suffering can range from mild to severe, from that which all of us experience as an expected part of living to those unusual forms of suffering experienced by only a few. But in any case, suffering results from excessive pain or discomfort and represents a holistic response to it involving body, mind, feelings, and faith.

How much suffering will occur in a given situation is determined more by how the person perceives the event than by the actual event itself. The breakup of a relationship, for example, is going to cause more suffering in the life of someone who perceives it as a major catastrophe than in the life of someone who sees it as a welcome release from an ill-advised commitment.

It's the same event for both people, yet, their perceptions are different. For one it's a disaster; for the other it's a blessing.

Suffering That Hurts

There are certain kinds of suffering that are particularly hazardous to the emotional health of children within the family. Let's consider a few of these. And again, while none of these situations may describe your family exactly, consider whether they reveal any tendencies you may have.

Some suffering in families is more emotionally harmful to developing children than other kinds.

Negative family climate. Some families create for themselves an internal family atmosphere of penitential suffering instead of one of redemptive celebration. Instead of celebrating life, in other words, they live it as a burden. Instead of looking in the mirror and seeing the image of the Creator, they see only sinful human nature. Where there's hope, they see despair. Where there's beauty, they often see ugliness. Where there's goodness, they're more likely to see inadequacy. These are parents who spend more time and energy looking for what's wrong in their children than celebrating what's good and right about them. The family focus, day in and day out, at virtually every encounter of parent and child, is to recognize and overcome personal weakness, flaws, and inadequacy. Unfortunately, many parents fall victim to the tendency of projecting their own weaknesses and faults upon their children, as though the children were nothing more than an extension of themselves, and then they feel compelled to punish the children as a way to correct the deficiency.

Children are neither all good nor all bad. There's an equal potential of good and evil in all things. Which we will see depends on which we're looking for. We tend to find what we expect. Parents who spend more time seeking the bad in people, their weaknesses, faults, and inadequacies, will generally find people to be bad, weak, and inadequate. Parents who believe the world is a hostile and dangerous place will teach their children to fear it. Such a perspective about themselves, other people, or the world around them can result in a serious mental and emotional handicap for children. It can seriously inhibit their thinking, feeling, and functioning.

Addictions. Chemical addictions occur when the body demands regular quantities of a particular substance such as alcohol in order to function smoothly. But just as damaging are psychological addictions that develop when we use certain forms of thinking or behavior as an emotional crutch—overeating, for example, as a method of achieving a feeling of personal comfort. The suffering of addictive parents can cause great distress in their children, who must stand by and watch helplessly as their parents self-destruct.

An addict is a slave to his addiction. He lives his life in service to it, constantly feeding and nurturing it, doing whatever is necessary to meet its endless demands. Addictive parents, as a result, often have little time or energy left over to spend with their children. The children must tend to their own needs as best they can. Besides exposing their children to senseless suffering over which they have no control and raising them in an environment of physical and emotional deprivation, addictive parents rarely present good parenting models for their children. Yet, children learn how to *be* parents by watching *their* parents. The harmful effects of poor parenting models will become evident when the children become parents themselves.

Chronic anxiety. Anxiety is fear without an obvious cause; it's an extremely foreboding sensation of dread as though something terrible is about to happen. But anxiety differs from fear in that there is no actual danger threatening. The stimulus of fear comes from without the individual; whereas the stimulus for anxiety originates within the person. In its most extreme form—panic—the symptoms are similar to those of fear and are obvious: increased pulse rate, increased muscular tension, palpitating, sweating, rapid breathing, dilated pupils, agitated behavior, and a sense of physical weakness. At less intense levels, anxiety is experienced as apprehension, uncertainty, restlessness, or dread—a mild to severe sense of danger, tragedy, or disaster. If the anxiety is repressed and not allowed physical or emotional expression, it may lead to a variety of psychosomatic symptoms including peptic ulcers, asthma, headaches, spastic colon, or high blood pressure. This is because the essential purpose of fear is to act as a warning signal to the individual that he faces an external danger. Anxiety is a similar sensation, or warning, that some threat is present within the individual. But since the inner danger is unconscious, it cannot be dealt with as can outer, realistic danger. The result is often repression, then, which creates its own problems for the person.

The roots of chronic anxiety lie in childhood. We know that the lack of a healthy emotional atmosphere within the family during the early years of life will likely hamper healthy personality development. We also know that the more emotional insecurity an individual feels during the formative years of childhood, the more anxiety he will experience as an adult. Our anxiety patterns are determined in early childhood when we perceive separation from our parents—our only source of warmth, food, and comfort—as very frightening. It instills within us a sense and feeling of insecurity and uncertainty. When we grow up and face the world with all its pressures, demands for change and sacrifice, adjustments, and other threats to our adult sense of personal security and self-worth, we experience a similar sense of anxiety.

Insecure, anxious parents tend to raise insecure, anxious children. They pass their suffering on to their children as a hidden legacy.

Parent burnout. Modern families are subjected to so much change, so much stress in their attempt to function successfully in a complex and demanding society, that burnout is a common problem among them. The word *burnout* comes from the concept of a rocket using up all its fuel. It's commonly used today to depict a sense of exhaustion and emotional depletion due to stress and the demands of living. Symptoms include extreme fatigue, irritability, the inability to work efficiently, poor appetite, feelings of apathy, and the inability to enjoy life in general.

It's exceedingly difficult for parents suffering from burnout to respond in positive, helpful ways to the special needs and concerns of their children. Instead, they tend to become hypercritical of even the smallest deviance from what they expect and then overreact with harsh words or punishment. These parents often feel too tired and too overwhelmed to care. They tend to withdraw emotionally from their children, leaving them to live and grow in an emotional wasteland.

Inferiority complex. A complex is a subconscious idea or group of ideas that influence our behavior beyond our control. We all have mild complexes of some kind. Unless they're rigid or destructive or interfere with day-to-day living, they cause little concern. They become a problem for us when they begin to interfere with our functioning.

One of the most damaging complexes is the inferiority complex. This is a pervasive feeling of physical, intellectual, or social inadequacy. We always fall short in comparison with other people. Or we're never good enough, smart enough, attractive enough. We just aren't enough.

Most inferiority complexes originate in the helplessness we feel as infants and small children in the family. The sense of inadequacy may persist and become even more of a problem for us if, as we grow up, we're either overprotected or neglected by our parents to the point that we don't learn to fend for ourselves and gain confidence from repeated successes in our activities and relationships. A sense of inferiority may make us set our goals too low, or it may make us overcompensate in some other important area of life, such as when a man assumes a macho role in order to compensate for his short height. Or it can make us compromise our values, our hopes and dreams. People suffering from extreme inferiority complexes often end up settling for what they can get rather than working for what they want.

Parents with inferiority complexes often raise children who are extremely self-conscious. Like their parents, they fear the attention of people. They're afraid that if people look too closely, they'll see the inadequacies they're sure are so much a part of them.

Chronic depression. All of us feel depressed from time to time, but usually not for very long. Emotional depression typically follows some environmental condition to which it's a response, such as the death of a close relative, an economic setback, or some other crisis that might ordinarily be expected to produce a temporary unhappiness, but not unhappiness to as severe a degree nor for as prolonged a period of time. Its most prominent symptoms are a chronic state of dejection or despondency, accompanied by a tendency toward self-depreciation. The depressed person may still be able to work and relate on a limited scale to the family, but typically the joys ordinarily derived from these activities are greatly diminished. The person no longer shows any zest or interest in the things he does but rather goes through them mechanically and almost automatically. The most threatening types of depression to the evolving emotional health of your children are those that become severe, that disrupt normal family life and functioning, that persist for weeks or months, or that become destructive or suicidal.

These are but a few of the kinds of suffering parents can experience that will almost inevitably have a negative effect on the health and development of children. A few others include extreme eating habits, extreme aversions, compulsions, delusions, exhibitionism, extreme guilt, hypochondria, jealousy, kleptomania, pathological lying, martyrdom, nightmares, obsessions, perfectionism, phobias, psychosomatic illnesses, voyeurism, and of course, violence.

The process of growing up and adapting to life is never entirely easy and comfortable, even under the best of circumstances. The most normal of us will go through occasional phases of emotional distress, such as temporary periods of anger at a family member or feelings of depression, of being misunderstood or of being persecuted. Yet if our early training and environment have been proper and healthy, we will soon overcome these difficulties, and our personalities will continue along their paths to maturity, fulfillment, and happiness.

The Importance of Effective Problem Solving

While it's not advisable to keep all problems hidden from your children, as a rule childhood should be as carefree as possible. What is most important is that your children witness effective problem solving by you when problems do occur. Learning that life and its difficulties are manageable is an important building block in mental and emotional health. It inspires hope.

All families have problems. What is important to the emotional health and development of your child is that he witness and participate in effective problem solving with you.

Effective problem solving begins by identifying the problem. Stop and think. Pinpoint the problem. Problems can't be solved if you don't know what they are or how to recognize them. The first step in any treatment for a problem of any sort is acknowledging that a problem exists. Be specific. Generalizations such as "I just don't feel good!" aren't enough.

Next, tell and listen. Get help! Talk to a friend or another family member, or seek professional counsel. But tell someone about the problem. Then listen to his response. Most problems aren't problems at all. More often, the problem is our perception. We blow things out of proportion or get defensive and look for reasons to be hurt or offended. Many of us actually seek out reasons to be unhappy! Specifically, discuss options you have in dealing with the problem.

Then, decide and act. Once you have discussed your options, choose one that best suits your needs and *act*. Don't wait. The best time to deal with a problem is immediately—as soon as possible. Problems have a way of getting worse or of provoking other problems if they go unattended long enough. Don't let yourself be a victim. Act quickly and decisively to resolve the problem.

Finally, evaluate. After the problem has been resolved and is no longer a threat, take a minute or two to evaluate how you handled the problem and the effectiveness of the action you chose. Be honest! If another course of action might have been more effective, acknowledge it. Your children need to learn how to solve problems effectively. They can learn this only from you.

Helping Your Child Cope

During those times when you're suffering, it's important that you help your child cope with the situation as best you can under the circumstances. Your goal should be to minimize the possibly harmful effects on your child. Some ways to do this might include the following:

1. Be honest. Openly acknowledge to your child that times are tough right now or that you have a problem you're struggling to overcome. You don't necessarily have to tell your child what the problem is, just that you have a problem you're trying to resolve.

2. Acknowledge the problem as being yours only. Make sure your child knows and understands that he's not the problem or the cause of it. Children so easily blame themselves for problems in the family. This could lead to other problems.

3. Ask your child for help. Tell him what he can do to help you as you work through the problem. Be specific! Maybe it's cleaning the kitchen tonight, being extra quiet, keeping the television turned way down, or going to bed earlier so that you can go to bed early. Most children will gladly cooperate as a way to "help" when they might not be so eager to "mind" you. A word of caution: be careful that you don't attempt to use your child as a

therapist. It's a mistake to turn to children for counsel and comfort in times of distress. At such times, what's needed is another adult.

4. Reassure your child. As best you can in the circumstances, assure him that everything is going to be all right. Try to maintain some sense of personal control while in the presence of the child. Children tend to become frightened and panicky when their parents are out of control.

5. Keep family life consistent. As best you can, maintain family roles, functions, and routines. Following normal patterns of family life can be a stabilizing factor in the midst of a crisis or other family problem. This can provide the structure children need in times of uncertainty.

6. Listen. If you're able, listen to your child express how he feels about what's happening. Children have feelings that need to be expressed also. This would be a good time to dispel unreasonable fears and anxieties while offering some reassurance.

7. Get help. If you're not able to help your child cope and if you see the situation is inhibiting his ability to think, function, and perform, get him some professional help. Don't wait until there's a crisis in his life! Remember, the goal at such times is to minimize any possible harm to your child.

Occasional problems are a natural part of life. All of us experience difficulties from time to time. Yet if our early training and environment have been proper and healthy, we will soon overcome them, and our personalities will continue along the path to maturity, fulfillment, and happiness.

Unfortunately, however, many people fail to make satisfactory adjustments between the needs and demands of their own personalities and those of the environment in which they live. These persons tend to be tense and in conflict as a result of unresolved childhood problems, and unless help is sought and they find ways to overcome their problems, they may become mentally ill.

Points to Remember

The emotional health of children is affected by the emotional health of their parents. Emotionally healthy parents tend to create positive, supportive home environments conducive to the emotional health and development of their children. Parents, for example, who don't take life and its problems too seriously and are able to laugh at themselves are likely to raise children better able to cope with life's problems and their own mistakes. Similarly, emotionally unhealthy parents tend to create a home environment that perpetuates and supports their problems, thereby exposing their children to the effects of those problems. Anxious and paranoid parents, for example, are likely to raise children who are overly cautious in relationships and always looking beyond the obvious to hidden intentions. They adopt their parents' fears of being exploited and becoming a victim of another's will or desire.

It is essential to the emotional health of your children that you be emotionally healthy. Thus, it is important that you tend to your own emotional needs and resolve any emotional conflicts you might have. Following are ten suggestions for doing so.

1. Be honest. Lives and relationships built on illusions are doomed to failure. Be honest with others and with yourself. Admit to personal problems and hang-ups, and do what's necessary to overcome them or at least limit their effect on others.

2. Know that there is often a difference between what you need and what you want. Seek the one and hope for the other. Meeting needs is essential for emotional health.

3. Expose yourself to people and events that enhance your emotional well-being rather than diminish it. Spend your time with positive, healthy people who enjoy life.

4. Provide yourself adequate breathing room and quiet time alone. It's important to know you can stop the world and get off for a moment's rest occasionally.

5. In times of stress, trouble, or crisis, seek help and support from people you trust. People need people. Adults have needs that only another adult can meet. When parents turn to their children to meet their adult needs, problems are sure to develop.

6. Learn about human behavior. Knowing why adults and children do the things they do will help you understand puzzling

or confusing behavior that might otherwise cause you distress or concern. Understanding often brings a sense of peace.

7. Be assertive. Speak your piece quietly and clearly. Doing so protects your sense of integrity, your dignity, and your rights. It prevents domination by others and the creation of a victim's mentality.

8. Know what's important and what isn't. Invest your time, energy, and attention only in those things most important to you, your family, or those around you. Learn to say no.

9. Cultivate and maintain a simple, enjoyable routine of diet, exercise, rest, and recreation. Your emotional well-being is closely related to your physical health.

10. Don't allow despair to take over your life. Maintain a faith in people. Seek the good in all things. The ability to trust is essential to emotional health. Remember that beauty and ugliness exist together. Pursue the good diligently.

Chapter 6
Silence Is Golden?

Imagine, for a moment, that you can't hear. Deaf since birth, you live in a world of total silence. You can't hear what's going on around you. You can't hear the phone or the doorbell ringing or the buzzer on the dryer telling you the clothes are dry. You can't hear what people around you are saying or those beautiful words of love and affection so many of us take for granted. You can't even hear the gurgles and cries and first words of your babies.

Now imagine what it must be like to be trapped by someone else's silence. A silence over which you have no control. A silence just as real as a wall made of brick and mortar. Imagine that you can hear, but that person won't speak. Could you build a life that's normal, happy, and full around this kind of silence? How much could you learn in a silence used to punish?

After her parents' divorce, five-year-old Susan found it harder and harder to talk with her mother. Her mother always seemed busy, preoccupied, or just too tired to talk or do the things with Susan that meant so much to her. Susan learned that it was better just to leave her mother alone at certain times instead of trying to talk to her. Like when she was really tired, depressed, or angry—one or another of which seemed to be most of the time now that her father was gone. Sometimes Susan would try to say something that would make her mother feel better during those times. But it never worked. More often than not, it only made her mother more angry or more depressed. Sometimes she would scream at Susan to go away and leave her alone. At other times she would just ignore her, pretending that Susan wasn't even there. Sometimes she would ignore her for hours, or even for a day or two.

It hurt Susan to see her mother suffering so much. It hurt her even more to think she was the cause of some of it. In order not to hurt her mother, Susan began withdrawing into her bedroom more and more. There she created a warm, happy world for herself with stuffed animals that became real, live, talking friends. In time, Susan became more comfortable in her fantasy world than in the world that existed outside her bedroom door. She spent almost all of her free time there. She had a wonderful time there. It was her home. She felt safe and secure there, and it had only happy, smiling faces in it.

In time, her mother adjusted to the divorce and even remarried. But try as she might to re-establish a close relationship with Susan, nothing worked. Although the child was obedient and responsive, something was missing. It was as though her mother had lost touch with the evolving person inside the little girl's body she recognized as her daughter. It was as though Susan, the person, was gone. Or hiding, maybe. There was a barrier between mother and daughter so thick that nothing she could do seemed to make any difference. It was obvious the child would rather spend her free time alone in her room than with her mother—or anyone else.

By the time Susan and her mother first came to see me, Susan was an extremely introverted and withdrawn child whose fantasy world was more real than any other world she knew. It was her way of protecting both herself and her mother. She was passive and apparently uncaring. Perhaps she dared not care. Her mother was desperate. The challenge for all of us was obvious. How were we to bridge the barrier of silence that existed between Susan and her mother? What was the key that would un-lock the prisons that kept them trapped in each other's silence?

The Nature of Silence

In spite of that grim (though, unfortunately, not-too-unusual) picture of silence, there are actually few things in life as wonderful as silence. A moment of silence can be a much welcomed respite for those who make their living with the spoken word, a refreshing pause for those who work immersed in noise. What hustled, bustled, and anxious parent doesn't treasure a brief period of peace and quiet after a long day on the job before tackling the chores of home and family life?

For many people, silence is magic—the stillness out of which thought takes action, ideas take root, and the new takes wing as an imagined possibility. For others it's only after life is stripped of its endless distractions of sight and sound, only when the mind must turn to itself for stimulation, and only when the inflated ego can be diminished enough to become submerged in the quiet stillness of silence that they're able to find life's greatest gift—themselves! For those most fortunate ones, silence can be a key to inner freedom.

But for others, silence is a prison. Not only does it keep one person locked away in his own private world, but it can also keep other people locked out in theirs. Such a silence doesn't bring freedom. It makes slaves of its victims, reducing life to an empty, lonely void where even a kind word becomes an invaluable prize. For such people, silence is not a blessing but a curse. It isn't something to be sought and treasured but is an evil to be avoided at all costs.

Silence can be a prison. It can be a barrier between you and your child as real as brick and stone.

This is the situation for many children, and not just in extreme cases like Susan's. Many parents, in fact, use silence occasionally if not all the time in ways that harm their children, and I would ask you again to examine your own parenting style for tendencies in this direction. If you recognize anything of yourself in the following pages and make some positive changes as a result, you and your children will all benefit.

Silence That Hurts

Some uses of silence do nothing to help children and a lot to hurt them. Instead of being a gift to strengthen and enlighten them, silence can become a tool that exploits their personal vulnerabilities. Few things are as frightening as our own weaknesses and inadequacies.

One wrongful use of silence is as a tool of manipulation. Consider the case of ten-year-old Sherry. Mother doesn't like to wash the dishes after dinner. Neither does Sherry. And who could blame them? Mother and daughter have a running battle over the issue that has lasted months. Mother wants Sherry to assume responsibilty for the dishes after every meal without having to be told to wash them. Sherry looks for every excuse to avoid having to do the chore.

Then one evening Mother changes her tactics. Instead of the usual confrontation scene after the meal, Mother sighs deeply, and with an air of great pain and sacrifice, she does the chore herself without a word spoken to Sherry. Initially, Sherry is pleased that she won't have to wash the dishes on this particular night. But not for long! Mother maintains her posture of injured silence toward Sherry all evening long, speaking to her only when Sherry speaks directly to her. Everything about Mother—her posture, her expressions and attitude, and her silence—combines to tell Sherry how hurt and disappointed she is that Sherry didn't do what was expected of her.

After a while, Sherry begins to feel guilty for disappointing her mother. The feeling of guilt grows slowly into worry as the wall of silence hanging between them doesn't disappear as the evening wears on. Instead, Mother seems to be withdrawing more and more. The uncertainty that now is a part of their relationship begins to frighten Sherry. As is the case with most children, one of her greatest fears is that her mother will stop loving her and won't want her any more. Now feeling terribly insecure and desperately needing Mother's approval again, Sherry begins to try to make amends for her earlier attitude. She pampers mother and vows to wash the dishes on the following evening.

Mother's goal was to get Sherry to assume responsibility for washing the dishes after meals. There's certainly nothing wrong with that. And Mother got what she wanted from Daughter. What's disturbing is how she went about it. In order to get Sherry to do what she wanted, Mother had to manipulate the child emotionally. She used silence to trigger guilt, fear, and enough insecurity to force Sherry into submission. This approach centered on the child's normal abandonment anxiety and brought it to the level of a fear. This was enough to cause Sherry to act in the only way she knew to overcome the fear—by giving in and doing what Mother wanted her to do. The key to survival for Sherry in this instance was to please her mother.

Putting a child in the position of having to earn parental love and acceptance is not only cruel but also breeds insecurity in a child. It places the worth of the child not on who and what he is as a person but simply on what he says or does that pleases the parent. The child's feelings of self-worth then come from other people rather than from within himself. Such teaching not only sets the child up to fail if he doesn't live up to other people's expectations, but it also fosters low self-esteem and provides fuel for later emotional problems.

Manipulated people rarely feel good about what's going on. More likely, they resent it and are angry. If the relationship is too important to jeopardize with an honest expression of feelings, as in Sherry's case with her mother, the child is likely to repress the feelings within a powerful whirlwind of internal conflict. If the internal conflict lasts long enough and is severe enough, it will make itself known nonverbally—through emotional, behavioral, and physical symptoms. Relationships of any kind that are based on repressed feelings of anger and hostility are never healthy.

Mother's wanting Sherry to help with the dishes after meals was entirely legitimate. But a less damaging approach is available. Consider the following scenario.

First, Mother needs to be careful to make sure she isn't expecting too much from her child. Most seven year olds are capable of helping with such a chore, but expecting Sherry to assume total responsibility for it without being told to is treating her like an adult, not a child. This is an unrealistic, inappropriate, and potentially harmful expectation.

Next, what do you think would have been Sherry's response if Mother had sat her down one evening and said, "Sherry, I have a problem, and I wonder if you could help me solve it. I need someone to help me with the dishes after meals. Do you think you could help me?"

Third, clearly identify the problem. The problem is that Mother wants help doing the dishes after meals.

Fourth, define clearly and precisely what "help" means. What specifically are you asking the child to do? In this case, Mother could say, "You can best help me by clearing all the dishes off the table, carrying them into the kitchen, wiping off the table, and then putting the dishes into the dishwasher after I rinse them off." Children can't live up to your expectations if they don't understand what those expectations are.

Then *ask* for the child's help and cooperation. *Telling,* in most instances, sets the child in conflict with the parent and results in resistance. On the other hand, most children have a deep need to please their parents and want to be helpful. Mother could have simply said to Sherry, "Can you do these things to help me?"

Sixth, when possible, give the child a choice. Children are more willing to do what they have chosen to do than what others tell them they must do. Mother could say, "Which would you rather do, clear the plates from the table or the silverware? Rinse the dishes or put them in the dishwasher? Wipe off the counters or the table?"

Seventh, compliment the child's attitude of helpfulness and his efforts, even though they may not be up to an adult standard. Rewarded behavior most likely will be repeated with the hope of receiving more of the reward.

Last, and perhaps most important of all, share the chore with the child. Build a feeling of camaraderie, of shared purpose, of cooperation. Children love to be a part of things. Sharing an experience with your child has more the effect of a gift. Imposing an experience has more the effect of a punishment.

Another wrongful use of silence is as a means of control through the threat of physical force. Once children have experienced the painful reality of physical punishment in their lives, they tend to sensitize themselves to its potential presence in every situation. As a result, some children reach a point of living to avoid punishment. When that happens, just the threat of it can have the same effect as the force itself. In such cases, silence can be used by parents as a form of intimidation designed to control their children.

Mark and Jerry were playing together in the bedroom one evening. In the midst of their playful wrestling on the floor, their father appeared at the bedroom door. He stood full in their view, his legs firmly planted apart, his arms crossed in front of him, and his eyes boring angrily into them. The boys stopped their play and stared expectantly at their father. They waited uncertainly for him to say something that would clarify his intentions. The boys weren't sure whether they were in trouble or not.

The longer their father stood there, silent and staring, the more uncomfortable the boys became. Like most children, they began to assume the worst. They were indeed in trouble and were about to be punished.

The silence hung heavily throughout the room, full of threats, triggering memories of other painful encounters the boys had had with their father and his belt when they were in trouble. Suddenly, the boys were scared and began to cry. Even though no blow had been struck, the effect on the boys was the same: they were willing to do anything to please their father and avoid the punishment.

103

Healthy and well-adjusted children rarely grow out of environments characterized by fear, pain, and suffering. Intimidation through the use of silence puts a barrier of doubt and uncertainty between the child and the parent. The child is never quite sure if the parent loves him enough not to hurt him. Feeling safe and secure in the relationship with his parents is essential for a healthy childhood. These feelings don't grow out of uncertainty and fear.

Effective parents don't control their children with threats, implied or explicit. They discipline them. There's a difference. Controlling children does little to teach them to control themselves. It teaches, instead, submission to those bigger and more powerful than themselves. It teaches passivity, highlights personal inadequacy and helplessness, and makes victims of children who can't defend themselves. It robs them of hope.

A third bad way to use silence is as punishment. One of the most common, yet damaging, forms of parental punishment is the withholding of love and affection, which usually occurs in the midst of parental silence. Most often, it's a silence characterized by assumed indifference, as though the child is no longer worthy of the parent's love and attention. The parent becomes unavailable to the child, distant, aloof, and removed from the situation at an emotional level. He tends to be unresponsive to the child, ignoring him or refusing to answer or look at him. This is similar in appearance to silence used to manipulate, except in this case the parent isn't trying to make the child do anything. He just wants him to feel bad.

The effect on the child is the same as if the parent physically pushed the child away and held him at arm's length. Children need their parents, up close and intimate. They need lots of physical and emotional contact, lots of nurturing. These are basic necessities of emotional health. Willfully depriving children of them as punishment is similar to depriving children of food and water for the same reason.

Silence used to manipulate, control, and punish is harmful silence and can emotionally impair your child.

Silence: Good or Bad

The ability to be alone, to be comfortable and at peace in the company of no one but oneself, to find meaning and purpose in solitude, and the willingness to come face to face with oneself without distraction are all essential aspects of emotional health. Children who come to know themselves are likely to find it easier to know others. Those who can live with themselves are likely to be better able to live with others. If children can find peace and purpose in solitude, they are likely to find an even greater peace and purpose in togetherness.

Parents who use silence as a weapon against their children, however—as a tool of manipulation or as a punishment—create an aversion to and fear of it in their children. These children experience it as painful and something to be avoided at all costs. The result is that they often spend more time and energy than is healthy pursuing relationships with people and ways to make sure they don't have to be alone, at least for very long. They cling to cliques, bury themselves in groups, and become distressed when something interferes with their social activity. Even when they're alone, they fill the room with the presence of other people through posters, pictures, the radio, and television.

Silence can be a creative process of growth and learning; a restorative pause in life's endless pursuits; a moment to catch one's breath, to take a closer look, or to listen with more than one's ears. Faith and the peace it brings grow not out of chaos

105

and confusion but from the stillness of a human heart and mind that are neither strangers nor have reason to fear each other.

But as with all God's gifts, parents must teach their children not only its proper use but also its value. Children aren't likely to value what isn't valued by parents. Nor are they likely to practice what their parents are unwilling to model. If silence is to be a valued part of human existence and the gateway to God and the self, it must be practiced routinely in the family. Parents must use it for its greatest good rather than for the immediate effect it can have in controlling their children.

Silence is golden only for those who know its possibilities. It can be used to imprison or to set free. It can bless a life or curse it. Which it does for the child will be determined by which it does for the parent.

Points to Remember

Silence is an important part of any life. It's essential to the emotional health of children that they learn to appreciate its possibilities and never know it as a frightening force in their lives. The following review and suggestions will help you use silence as a creative, constructive force in the lives of your children.

1. Begin early in the lives of your children teaching them the value and importance of silence. Remember that children tend to value and consider important what parents value and consider important.

2. Never use silence to punish or control your children. Doing so only makes them avoid it and perhaps even fear it. People who are afraid to be alone tend to be people who will pay almost any price not to be alone.

3. Try to have a period each day for quiet time. Maybe a half-hour, or even ten minutes, before bedtime. Encourage your children to use it for thinking over what has occurred during the day, the things that made them feel good, the events that made them feel bad, what they would do differently if they could, or for thinking about all the good things they have in their lives and

the many reasons they have to be happy. They can then say a prayer of thanks to God for those things.

4. Teach your children how to be comfortable in silence by doing it yourself. Quiet time becomes most beneficial in the family when it becomes routine, an anticipated event each day. But your children will do it only if you do it.

5. Be careful to respect the privacy of your children during quiet time, just as you want them to respect your privacy. Allow them to have their time and space uncontrolled and uninvaded by you.

6. Take five minutes after each quiet time to discuss with each other the value gained from it. Describing its value in your own life will help them recognize its value for themselves.

7. Invite your children to additional periods of silence as they grow and mature. Teach them other uses for it, such as reading, study, and other kinds of prayer.

Part 2
The Well-Adjusted Child

Chapter 7
The Well-Adjusted Child

I will never forget Tiny. Or how we met. I was twenty years old and had just started my first semester of classes at a local junior college. I was accepted into a work/study program that placed me in a ghetto elementary school as a part-time teacher's assistant. It was my first day on the job. After spending the morning in the classroom, I was assigned playground duty while the teachers had lunch.

I had hardly stepped onto the playground when I was surrounded by a swarm of curious children wanting to know who I was, why I was there, and if I had any chewing gum. It was while I was busy trying to answer their endless questions that Tiny made his way through the bustling crowd until at last he was standing almost directly in front of me. The top of his head barely reached my waist. Talking with the other children, I paid no attention to the brown, shiny face staring up at me.

For a moment he stood there. Then it happened! Tiny and I met each other face to face. With all the strength he could find in his little body, Tiny reached up and hit me in the groin. As I doubled over from the pain, the other children made a path, and Tiny scampered off as fast as his churning little legs would carry him. With only one thought burning in my mind, it took only a few seconds for my long legs to outstride his short ones. Needless to say, Tiny and I had a little heart-to-heart chat right there in the middle of the playground. After a heated discussion, Tiny and I reached an agreement: I would not wring his neck, and he would never hit me again!

From that day onward—as strange as this may seem—Tiny and I became friends. He was my constant shadow and ally the full two years I worked in the school.

As Tiny took a special interest in me, I took a special interest in him. I soon learned that Tiny had problems. His father was serving time in a state penitentiary, while his mother struggled to support her family of six children. The family was poor—very poor. Tiny and his brothers and sisters were pretty much on their own to take care of themselves. He spent most of his free time on the streets. He hated cops, particularly white cops—or any white authority, for that matter. A white cop had arrested his father and a white judge and jury had sentenced him to prison.

Tiny's problems at home carried over into the classroom. All the teachers knew him to be a poor student, quick-tempered and arrogant. Most had written him off as an incorrigible who would stay in school only until he was old enough to drop out or until he got into trouble with the law. It's not that the teachers didn't try to teach him. They did. The problem was that Tiny made no effort to learn. He was more preoccupied with other matters. Tiny was riding a fast train to self-destruction.

But then we organized the football team. Every boy in the school wanted to be on that team! They would do anything for a chance to compete. Even study. And not fight in the halls or on the playground. They would even stop smoking in the restrooms and running the streets at night. It was incredible the change that came over Tiny and so many of the other children in that school. Attitudes changed. Behavior changed. Grades were brought up. Even Tiny began to perform in class. School now came to mean more than just classes, bossy teachers, and homework for the kids. It became "their" school.

At the end of my two years at the school, the team had a combined 23–1 record and was city champion both years. Tiny had changed from street fighter to one of the best wide receivers in the city. His grades had improved from *D*'s and *F*'s to *B*'s and *C*'s, and he had become a favorite among the teachers and other students.

Although I wasn't able to watch as Tiny moved on into junior high school and then high school, I did learn several years later that he not only graduated from high school, but he did so with honors, and he was also a high school all-American football player! Who would have thought that little guy who hit me that first day at the school could do so well?

As was clearly the case with Tiny, later life grows out of early life. Adulthood is built on childhood. Children do not merely grow into adults. They simply become more of what they are, which, when combined with age, equals adulthood. Beliefs and attitudes fashioned in childhood will likely become the bases of adult decisions. Habits started in childhood are likely to be carried into adulthood. Unresolved childhood problems and conflicts will also be carried into adulthood, where they will take on adult proportions with adult consequences.

Most of us attempt to create a childhood for our children that reflects its magic, joys, and infinite possibilities while protecting them as best we can from its many hurts and disappointments. We encourage our children to experience fully all that childhood has to offer, knowing that the rest of their lives depends on what's found there.

Yet we all know that childhood has its problems—lots of them! Some are a necessary part of human growth and development. Others are totally unnecessary. Some problems are self-created. Others are created for us by people whom we love and respect. Still others result from activities and relationships outside the family.

Regardless of their source, all childhood problems have one thing in common: they result in internal and external conflict in a child. They're often painful and distressful. Most damaging are the internal conflicts. These are conflicts that tend to pit the child against himself or the authority of a parent or a teacher. This is conflict that arises, for example, when what the child wants to do is not what he believes he ought to do in a particular situation. The result is a feeling of being split, at odds with himself, of being torn between pleasing self or pleasing others, knowing either choice will involve a personal sacrifice of some sort.

All childhood problems have one thing in common: they create great internal and external stress for the child.

Emotional damage can result for the child if internal conflict is not resolved successfully. It can distort the personality and affect the rest of the child's life. Well-adjusted, healthy children who thrive are those who successfully resolve their developmental conflicts.

Understanding Developmental Conflicts

Under normal conditions, life is a series of developmental stages that begin at conception and continue throughout adulthood. Each stage involves certain developmental tasks that must be mastered if growth is to continue normally. Because of the complexity of these tasks and the changes they force on a child, they often create high levels of anxiety, stress, and conflict that may become noticeable as emotional symptoms. This is normal and to be expected. But if the child is to continue growing emotionally, these conflicts must be resolved before beginning the next stage of development.

114

If the tasks are *not* mastered at the appropriate stage of development, the child is likely to suffer immaturities and incompetencies that compound as he moves on through succeeding stages. Each new stage is entered with the legacy of past stages. Weak points in character contributed by earlier developmental failures will influence, if not jeopardize, successful development in the current stage.

How well your child deals with developmental problems and conflicts will be largely determined by how you as his parent react to them. Certain parental responses at these particularly vulnerable times can aggravate an age-appropriate conflict into a developmental crisis for your child. Thus it's no surprise that well-adjusted children have parents who are knowledgeable about the stages of emotional development and just as concerned about growth in that area as they are about physical, intellectual, and social development. The discussion that follows will help you better understand these stages.

Stage One: The First Year of Life

The essential task of this stage is for your child to develop a sense of trust about life, the world around him and, most especially, his parents. The quality of this parent-child relationship will form the basis of every future relationship for him.

The child is more helpless during this stage of development than he will ever be again. He must trust and depend on others, particularly his parents, for all things, food, shelter, warmth, nurturing, protection, reassurance, and so on. It's essential that you be aware of this and not betray your child's trust to provide all he needs.

If the physical and emotional needs of the child are met by a close, attentive, and nurturing parent, the child will develop a sense of security, of being safe and protected in his world. A trusting world view and the capacity to trust other people are essential to the well-adjusted, thriving child.

In addition to being able to trust his parents for basic life necessities a child in this stage must gain some sense of the meaningfulness of human life and activity. He must come to believe there is a reason parents do and say the things they do and that this reason has his best interests in mind. It's not enough that you develop a method of guiding and controlling him through a system of prohibitions and permissions, a series of do's and don'ts. He needs to realize there is meaning to it all and that your intentions can be trusted. If this doesn't happen—if he learns instead that he can't trust the intentions of those who have some control over his life—the consequences in adulthood, when he must work for an employer, be part of an institution, or enter into a marriage, can be devastating.

Some ways of helping your child accomplish the essential task of this stage might be to . . .

. . . respond promptly when your baby cries. For children this young, crying is the only form of communication they have available. If crying doesn't bring an appropriate response from you, your child is trapped by his inability to communicate his needs. Responding quickly teaches your child he can trust you to take care of him.

. . . tend promptly to your baby's needs. Feed him and change his diapers as needed. Keeping your baby clean and comfortable physically facilitates emotional comfort and security as well.

. . . give your child lots of physical and emotional intimacy. Touch him and talk to him as much as possible. Not only does this stimulate growth and development in your child, but it likewise helps in the bonding process that is essential to a healthy parent-child relationship.

. . . keep the environment as constant as possible during the early months of your child's life. Try to limit the amount of change your child must adapt to during this period. Familiar faces, places, and objects that don't change from day to day help your child feel comfortable, safe, and secure in his new world.

Stage Two: The Second Year of Life

The primary task for your child during this stage is to achieve a basic sense of personal autonomy, to be able to perceive and understand himself as separate and distinct from his parents, with a mind, body, and will of his own. The crucial skills to be developed during this stage are in the area of decision making. A child must learn to manipulate and discriminate between options, and then develop the capacity to make a choice. Your child will gain the needed sense of autonomy through making choices for himself and having those choices respected by you, his parent.

The difference between ability and disability is often parental permission to try during the early years. Children encouraged to try will develop abilities. Those punished for trying will learn disabilities.

On the other hand, repeated failure in his decision-making attempts during this stage through punishment or discouragement from you may teach him instead a deep sense of helplessness and incompetence, which results in feelings of personal shame and self-doubt. He may learn to distrust his decision-making powers, and an unhealthy dependence on other people may develop, which could set him up to be controlled by the wills of other people.

Some ways of helping your child achieve the goals of stage two might be to . . .

. . . recognize your child's ambivalence. The second year of life can be especially painful for your child because he remains almost totally dependent upon you and yet is driven to seek independence. Allow him to try, and fail if necessary, within an environment of understanding and compassion.

. . . allow your child to make some decisions. This can best be done in that area of free choice discussed in Chapter 4. Choosing what clothes to wear while at home, which glass to use for a drink, and which book to read are activities with no risk to the child's health or welfare. Yet allowing your child to make these choices and experience their consequences, both positive and negative, can be very beneficial to his mental and emotional development.

. . . allow your child to do for himself. This is the age at which most children want to start doing things for themselves, such as dressing and feeding themselves. Children learn competency and self-adequacy from attempting and successfully completing tasks.

. . . be encouraging, patient, and kind as your child tries, awkwardly at first, to do those things for himself that you could do so much more easily and with a great deal less mess and fuss. Growing up is as tough a job as parenting.

Stage Three: The Third through Fifth Years of Life

The primary task of this stage is for your child to achieve a basic expression of initiative and responsibility, the ability to initiate activities without the prompting or help of you his parents, and to bring them to a successful completion. It isn't very important at this point how well a child completes a task. What is more important to his development is that he learn he can do it without assistance from a parent. Parents must be careful not to judge the results of their children's efforts by adult standards.

The danger of this stage is the sense of personal guilt and inadequacy that can result from failed attempts at doing things, performing tasks, or assuming responsibility for certain household chores. This becomes particularly acute in cases where the child fails to meet parental expectations and is punished. If your child's failures are exaggerated by punishment, he will experience considerable guilt at not being what you, the parent, wanted him to be, and he may resign himself to a level of personal inadequacy and incompetence. Later in life, such a child will not even try because he believes he can't achieve what is expected.

Some ways of helping your child accomplish the developmental goals of stage three might be to . . .

. . . recognize his need to attempt tasks without your assistance. This is an age of great curiosity and of wanting to imitate parents in activities and behavior. Doing things for himself gives him practice at being like you.

. . . allow your child to initiate, perform, and complete certain tasks that aren't threatening to his safety or that of others. Many times he will express frustration as he struggles against his own awkwardness in attempting the tasks. This is normal and healthy. Be patient and tolerant of his efforts. Don't take over the task when the going gets tough.

. . . provide as many opportunities for your child to try and succeed as possible. Success breeds confidence and a desire to continue. Repeated failures provoke feelings of discouragement and despair. Assign the child small tasks you are sure he can achieve with relative ease and for which he can earn some praise.

. . . be sure to reward successes consistently at this age. But don't punish failures. Punishment for trying at this stage could cause your child to maintain a "safe" posture that is passive and unwilling to try at all.

Stage Four: Approximately the Sixth through Twelfth Years of Life

A child's primary task in this stage of development is to achieve a basic expression of productivity and achievement, both at school and at home. In this stage, your child learns to win recognition and praise by producing things. This experience teaches him to be a worker and a potential provider and rewards him with social acceptance.

By this time, your child has mastered his ambulatory and sensory skills through play. Now he is ready to use these skills and tools in a more productive form of human activity—work. He develops a sense of industry.

If your child despairs of his tools and skills, thinking they're inadequate, or of his status among other children at his same developmental level, he will tend to abandon hope for the ability to identify with peers attempting to accomplish similar goals; he will feel personally inadequate; and he may develop an inferiority complex. Such a feeling of inferiority can cause great suffering in adult life.

Some ways of helping your child through stage four might be to . . .

. . . recognize this as the stage for "doing" lots of things. It's the time when your child is ready to apply what he's learned from watching you accomplish things around the house and in the yard.

. . . allow your child to "do" tasks. Let him start *and finish* the activity. Some good options here would be chores such as washing dishes, washing the car, folding the laundry, and so on. Be careful to assign chores your child is capable of completing successfully.

. . . allow your child to "make" things. This is a creative age when your child's imagination is alive with possibilities. Making toys, crafts, games, and other objects gives him a chance to integrate his natural curiosity and desire to do with a creative potential so important in later, adult life.

. . . praise his efforts. Even when the end result of an attempt to cook a meal or rearrange his room is not to your liking, praise both his intentions and his effort. Personal guilt should never accompany failure at this age, only an encouragement to try again.

Stage Five: Approximately the Thirteenth to Eighteenth Years of Life (Adolescence)

With the establishment of a healthy relationship to the world and with the people who occupy it, the development of skills and tools, and the beginning of sexual maturity, childhood comes to an end. Youth begins. This is a time in which children are primarily concerned with what they appear to be in the eyes of others compared to what they feel they are and with the question of how to connect the roles and skills cultivated earlier with an occupation and life pursuit.

The primary task of this stage is the establishment of a primary identity as a person. Successful development leads to the basis of a clear adult identity with an understanding of essential roles. Unsuccessful development leads to a scattered, fragmented, diffuse, and shifting sense of who and what one is as a person. A young person's identity tends to change with the situation and the demands being placed upon him. The result is that a typical adolescent remains a stranger even to himself.

The task of settling on an identity is so hard and so fraught with fear and uncertainty that young people often overidentify with the heroes of cliques and groups. They lose their own identity by assuming the group identity as a way to relieve their uncertainty and as protection from anxiety and self-doubt. It becomes a much-welcomed escape. Over a long enough time, it can become a trap.

There are no easy ways to negotiate adolescence. It's a tough, trying time for every child and parent. However, some suggestions for helping your child accomplish the task of finding his own unique identity are to . . .

. . . be as patient and compassionate as possible with your child as he struggles so painfully with his constantly changing self-image and his roles both in and out of the family. Sometimes in order to find out who they are, children during this stage feel a need to become the opposite of what their parents expect as a way of counterbalancing parental influence. It's a time when your child needs as much understanding and support as you can give.

. . . allow him to socialize. Provide opportunities for your child to be involved with other children of the same age in safe, controlled situations where there's no threat of personal exposure and being put on the spot. Organized group activities are ideal.

. . . provide opportunities to be involved. Every child has special interests, talents, and abilities that can be developed into something special for the child and perhaps even those around him. It's important that you give your child every opportunity not only to discover his special interests and abilities but to develop them as well. Maybe it's becoming a volunteer in a nursing home or through the Red Cross. Or maybe it's Boy or Girl Scouts, athletics, a chess club, a math club, or some other special interest group. About the only way to find what interests your child most and what he might be able to excel at is through trial and error.

. . . be a strong model. Children at this age desperately need strong adult examples. Much of learning who and what you are as a person comes through the often painful process of comparing yourself to others. Strong, healthy models are needed to facilitate this process of development.

. . . applaud his positive qualities. Try to keep your focus on what is right with your child during this trying time. It can be a great source of comfort to him to know that you accept who he is despite his problems.

The well-adjusted, thriving child has developed the following characteristics by resolving his developmental conflicts.

• He has a general trust of life, people, and the world around him.

• He is an autonomous individual capable of making responsible choices.

• He is a basically assertive person, initiating activities and assuming responsibility for them.

• He is a productive person, capable of achieving goals.

• He is a person with an identity, a sense of who and what he is as an individual.

Well-Adjusted Children Manage
Childhood Anxieties

Because of their basically helpless nature, children are even more vulnerable to life's many surprises and problems than are their parents. Their world is filled with doubts and uncertainties. Without strong, consistent support and protection from parents they can trust, children can become submerged in a seething pool of their own fears and nightmares.

Healthy, thriving children tend to be those who get proper nutrition, plenty of physical exercise, and lots of rest, and they have the strong support and encouragement of their parents. They are children who tend to manage well their childhood anxieties.

Typical childhood fears include the following:

Parents. Nothing is more important to the health and development of children than the relationship they have with their parents, as has been noted earlier. Most children have some desperate sense of the need to win parental acceptance and approval. Failure to do so can leave them rejected and abandoned. Well-adjusted, thriving children, however, experience low levels of anxiety regarding their parents.

School. School can be a great source of fear for children. Not only must they adjust to changing people and settings every year, but they must also adjust to changing demands and expectations. They must prove themselves adequate academically by passing an endless array of tests, and they must also prove themselves adequate in human relations. Such demands can only heighten fears of rejection, inadequacy, incompetence, and failure. But well-adjusted, thriving children tend to have low levels of anxiety concerning their performance at school.

Human relations. In addition to concern about parents, children are extremely sensitive to the expectations of other adults in their lives. It's vitally important to them to win acceptance and approval. To do this, they must be what the adults want them to be. Oftentimes this can create serious conflict, as when a teacher wants them to sit still, be quiet, and learn. The gym, dance, music, and theater instructors want children to be vocal, to be physically and emotionally demonstrative, and to perform. The police, principal, and relatives want them to be passive, obedient, and nonaggressive. The athletic coach, however, again wants them to take the initiative, to be determined and aggressive. And so it goes. There's a seemingly endless list of possibilities in terms of what adults expect children to be like, and children must try to please them all! Still, well-adjusted, thriving children have low levels of anxiety in this regard.

123

Crowding. Children are often crowded into limited spaces with lots of other children in day-care centers, classrooms, restrooms, playgrounds, recreational facilities, and so forth. This means children must limit their own personal space and must get along well with others—lots of them—and not be so possessive of what is theirs and theirs alone that conflict results from the inability to share. They must also compete for what they want and need with these other children. It's hard to get attention or to feel special in a crowd of many other children. This can be particularly devastating to children with low self-images who need attention in order to feel accepted. Well-adjusted, thriving children find constructive ways to stand out in a crowd, ways that bring them the praise and attention they desire.

Boredom. Boredom is the curse of childhood. Every child has experienced it from time to time, and every child hates it. Children need physical, intellectual, and emotional stimulation, and lots of it. They need to be challenged, awed, surprised, and rewarded through opportunities provided for learning and growth. Well-adjusted, thriving children can find challenges that keep them involved in what's happening around them. They experience low levels of boredom.

Loneliness. Lonely children aren't happy children. Every child needs the warmth and caring that come from close, personal relationships. During the early years of life, the only source of nurturing they have is their parents. Children deprived of fulfilling intimacy with their parents because the parents are too busy or too absorbed in their own problems tend to be lonely children. Well-adjusted, thriving children have close, intimate, and satisfying relationships, especially with one or both parents.

Relocation. One of the realities of our day and age is that families move. Parents find jobs, quit jobs, and find other jobs. For children this means lots of moving, from city to city, home to home, school to school. It means losing friends and making new ones. It means learning again where all the light switches are, the path to the bathroom in the dark, the location of their parents' room. It means change. There's little security for children in a world that constantly changes. Well-adjusted, thriving children rarely have to deal with the serious changes brought about by relocation. When they do move, their parents are especially sensitive to their needs and take steps such as those outlined in Chapter 1 to minimize the problems caused by the move.

Catastrophe. Disasters occur in every family from time to time. They usually come suddenly and bring great changes to the family. But not all families react to them in the same way. Some panic, creating other crises that leave them overwhelmed. Others are able to keep cool and calm and so limit the effects of the catastrophe on the family. Children need parents to help them interpret and understand strange and unusual events that occur in the family, particularly when they result in a family crisis. Left to their own interpretations, children are likely to imagine anything, most of which will certainly be self-destructive. Well-adjusted, thriving children have parents who can help them understand what's happening in a family crisis and provide models for coping with it. (For a fuller discussion of this, refer back once again to Chapter 1.)

Well-Adjusted Children Can Cope
with Life's Problems

Well-adjusted, happy children don't avoid life's problems. All children have problems. Rather, they have learned to handle their problems in socially acceptable and constructive ways, regardless of what the problem may be. With the support of their parents, these kids are in control—not of the problem itself, but of their response to it. Many childhood problems are just a natural part of growing up. But they can certainly be managed or, in some cases, mismanaged. How well kids manage their problems will be largely determined by how well their parents manage theirs. Like well-adjusted adults, children who have learned effective problem-solving skills from the example of their parents will acknowledge the problem, accept it for what it is, consider alternative solutions, make a decision, and then follow through on that decision.

Also like adults, children who perceive a threat in their lives that results in a crisis involving the use of coping skills have four basic responses to the threat:

1. Fight response: confront, attack, and overcome the threat directly.
2. Flight response: run and avoid the threat.
3. Denial response: simply ignore the threat or deny its existence.
4. Coexist response: make no effort to deal with the threat at all.

Healthy, thriving children tend to find ways to cope with those problems in their lives over which they have no control and cannot change. They also tend to find ways to solve those problems that can be resolved. These children rarely perceive themselves as helpless or as victims of life and its problems.

Coping children demonstrate five basic qualities:

1. They can concentrate. Problem solving involves the capacity to eliminate from one's thoughts those things not important to the issue, to focus one's attention on the problem and hold it there long enough to consider solutions and make a choice.

2. They can tolerate frustration. Children who cope best with life's problems have learned how to deal with not always having things go right. It helps them persevere despite the frustration that makes them want to give up until at last a solution is found.

3. They can postpone gratification. Kids who can postpone getting what they want and the rewards they seek are those who control the level of frustration, tension, and anxiety in their lives. Their ability to cope is enhanced when these stay within manageable limits.

4. They can communicate. Coping children can usually express themselves clearly and with some degree of precision to another person. Sharing their problems with others has great

therapeutic effect and helps them to put the problem into words so they're not overwhelmed by it and so it can be more easily understood and managed.

5. They can seek help. Well-adjusted children are not afraid to reach out for help when needed. They trust people enough to care. Such a capacity is essential in that it keeps them from feeling helplessly trapped within their own troubled world. Feelings of entrapment generally lead to panic, which will only intensify the crisis and perhaps even create others.

Well-Adjusted Children Have a High Level of Self-esteem

Children who thrive feel good about themselves. They feel loved, wanted, special, and competent both within the family unit and outside it. Their good feeling about who and what they are and their achievements is nurtured daily through positive feedback from friends, teachers, life events, and most decisively, their parents.

Children with healthy levels of self-esteem tend to demonstrate the following characteristics:

1. They are self-accepting. These children accept who and what they are as well as the circumstances of their lives. They spend little time trying to be what everyone else wants them to be. They feel accepted by their parents and other key people in their world, and consequently they find it easier to accept themselves, both their strengths and weaknesses.

2. They are individualistic. These kids are not hesitant to think for themselves or to act independently. They trust their own judgment and have enough self-confidence to be assertive and take the initiative. They don't need to prove themselves to others and don't feel strong needs to please as a way to win approval.

3. They are feeling people. These children aren't afraid to allow themselves to feel—whether pain, joy, sadness, happiness, love, or anger. They feel secure enough with themselves and their world to allow emotional responses to events and people.

4. They are able to express feelings. These children not only allow themselves to feel, but they are able and willing to express these feelings. They're not afraid of rejection if they're honest about how they feel. Nor are they out of touch with their feelings.

5. They are self-motivated. Children who feel good about themselves and their possibilities need little prompting. They tend to have eager, searching minds and imaginations. They initiate activity and relationships. They are also able to bring important activity to a successful conclusion with little supervision.

6. They don't fear failure. They have the courage to try, whether they succeed or fail. These children understand failing to be a part of the learning process and not a sign of personal inadequacy or weakness. They are willing to take the risk of failing in an attempt to succeed. They believe in themselves and their capabilities.

7. They generally like and trust people. These kids aren't afraid to get to know strangers in appropriate settings. They see other people as basically good and well intentioned. They are respectful, friendly, and sociable.

8. They tend to respect authority. Most of these children have only known fair and loving authority in their lives from parents and other significant adults. They have learned that they can trust the intentions of authority figures to have their best interests at heart. With trust comes respect.

9. They have low levels of guilt. These children perceive childhood mishaps as mistakes, as learning opportunities rather than crimes deserving punishment. When they have been willfully disobedient, they have experienced the joy of forgiveness. They understand, too, that there is a difference between the person and what the person might say or do.

10. They tend to have a high level of empathy with the thoughts, feelings, and behavior of other people. They are capable of putting themselves into the shoes of other people and are therefore more understanding of others and less judgmental of

their mistakes. They have little need to build themselves up by contrasting their qualities with others' weaknesses.

11. They are generally nonviolent. Children who feel good about themselves and other people tend to be less suspicious of others, don't seek conflict, and are less aggressive both verbally and physically. They have nothing to prove. When conflict does occur, they are more capable of finding nonviolent solutions.

12. They have an inner fulfillment. These children possess an inner peace, a contentment that can only come from knowing that all is well and as it should be. It's a sense of peace that comes from knowing their world is in order and they are masters of their world, at least to some extent.

Healthy children don't grow out of unhealthy childhoods. Punishing children for being normal doesn't stimulate normal growth and development. Well-adjusted children are those blessed with healthy childhoods in well-adjusted families.

Well-adjusted, healthy children manage their childhood anxieties, cope effectively with life's problems, and have a high level of self-esteem.

Chapter 8
Families That Thrive

Have you ever known a family you really envied? I have! They were an average income family, so I didn't envy them for their money, for a big, beautiful house, for luxury cars, or for fine clothes. I envied them because they seemed so happy.

They lived only two doors down the street. Both parents worked during the day while the two children were in school. They were undoubtedly the most popular people in the neighborhood. People just seemed to like them. Maybe it was because he was always available to lend a neighbor a hand with installing that new water heater or fixing the car. Maybe it was because she knew every child in the neighborhood by first name and always seemed to have a flock of kids in the front yard playing kick ball or hide-and-seek. Maybe it was because she seemed to care so much when anyone was sick or hurt or just needed someone to talk to. Or maybe it was just because they were so nice to everyone. They never seemed to have a bad word to say about anyone. What was even more impressive, they never seemed to have a bad word to say about each other.

Not once in all the time I lived down the street from them did I hear an unkind word from them about anyone. Except for an occasional complaint about the heat during summer and the cold during winter, I never once even heard them complain about anything! And yet they surely faced the same kinds of trials and tribulations encountered by every young family trying to get ahead in life. The children went to school and had homework like all the kids in the neighborhood. Occasionally, they, too, would come down sick with the flu or a cold. They had their music and dance lessons after school, along with the ball practices during the week and games on weekends. They were a very busy, normal family, just like all the others in the neighborhood. What made them so extraordinary was that they seemed to handle all the stress of everyday life so well! They were truly the most well-adjusted family I have ever met.

Just as important, every member of the family seemed well-adjusted. I remember wondering then how it was possible for four people to live together in the same house for so long and still be happy. Somewhere in the back of my mind I assumed that parents and children inherently don't get along, that growing up and being happy aren't possible at the same time.

It wasn't until much later that I learned that adult personalities are shaped by childhood experiences. Some of human behavior is the result of heredity, but most is learned. Attitudes, values, and beliefs that shape personalities are learned from experiences between parent and child. Indeed, the home environment and the relationship with his parents provide the foundation for all future relationships and the child's view of the world around him. How the child perceives the world will largely determine how he attempts to interact with it.

The home environment and the relationship with his parents are the two most powerful forces that shape a child's personality. It's important that both are healthy.

It's no accident that certain children thrive while others around them don't. Thriving children tend to have thriving parents, a healthy relationship with them, and a home environment that's not only secure but is also on the one hand a laboratory for exploring possibilities and on the other a clinic for healing. It provides a healthy atmosphere, an environment of responsibility while inspiring learning and growth, a therapeutic environment that brings healing and wholeness to broken, bruised, and hurting emotions. It's an environment that emphasizes physical, mental, emotional, and spiritual growth equally, not one at the expense of others. It doesn't fracture or fragment but makes whole.

Years later as I tried to understand what made that family down the street so different from my own, I came to realize that there's a difference between thriving and surviving. Whereas my family functioned at a survival level, the family down the street was thriving. I also learned that thriving families have certain characteristics.

Thriving Families Have
Well-Adjusted Parents

Well-adjusted, healthy, thriving children tend to have well-adjusted, healthy, thriving parents. These are people who have resolved their own developmental conflicts and have settled into a life with purpose that enables them to raise children and pursue life's greatest rewards.

Well-adjusted parents demonstrate some or all of the following qualities:

They have their personal lives under control. These parents lead well-balanced, constructive lives. They are economically stable, pursuing full-time jobs or careers. They maintain a permanent home and permanent social relationships. They are reasonably mature people with healthy self-esteems who have developed constructive ways of coping with and resolving conflict, along with life's many problems. They have deep commitments to the family while at the same time maintaining healthy interests outside it. They don't abuse drugs or alcohol.

They have accepted the child. Not every child is wanted and accepted by his parents. There are those who, from the parents' perspective, should never have been born. Many of these parents see their task of raising the child as a burden, something they have to do whether they want to or not—just another of life's endless, awful demands.

Well-adjusted parents, on the other hand, tend to have had good bonding experiences with their children at the time of birth. They relinquish the prebirth fantasy for the reality they now hold in their arms. They accept their children's appearance, sex, and physical characteristics even though they may differ from what they had wanted or imagined. They take the time to get to know each child as one stranger might another. They accept each child as a unique individual and welcome him into their lives as a new member of their family. When accepting the child, they also accept responsibility for his care.

They have prepared for parenthood. Parenting is a skill to be learned and developed. Well-adjusted parents have prepared themselves physically, emotionally, and intellectually for their child and the task of raising him. They have prepared a room in their home for him and furnished it with the necessities of any nursery. They have protected the health of their own bodies through adequate rest, nutrition, and exercise, and prenatal medical care. They have taken the time to learn about the changes that will occur in their lives, their family, and their relationships, and they have made the necessary emotional adjustments to accept these changes and challenges. They have also taken the time and made the effort to learn as much about babies and children as possible—everything from the actual birth process to feeding, changing, bathing, stimulating the child to normal development, and teaching and disciplining the child. Informed, knowledgeable parents make fewer mistakes.

They have reasonable expectations. One of the most common causes of physical and emotional injury to children is unrealistic parental expectations. Parents often expect too much too soon from their children. These are parents who have not taken the time to learn the developmental capabilities of children at any given age and therefore expect them to perform at a level beyond their ability. Such parents set their children up to fail. Failing, like any other form of human activity, can become a habit, a way of life.

Well-adjusted parents know what they can expect from their children at any particular age and are careful to keep their expectations within those limits. They provide endless opportunities for their children to succeed, to win their acceptance and approval. If failing can become a learned habit, so can succeeding!

In addition, these are parents who accept their children's mistakes as normal, natural, and expected. They experience them as opportunities for teaching and learning, not as crimes in need of punishment.

They use discipline rather than punishment. Children who thrive typically have parents who understand the difference between discipline and punishment and generally don't approve of or accept the use of harsh punishment in the parent-child relationship. They understand that punishment is an act of revenge that tears the child down, whereas discipline is an act of teaching that builds the child up. These parents tend to come from backgrounds themselves in which discipline rather than punishment was used.

They protect the child from excessive stress. Children experience as much stress and suffer from its symptoms as often as adults do. Kids can't thrive physically, emotionally, intellectually, or socially under conditions of excessive stress. It's critical to their growth and development that parents control the amount of stress in their lives and teach them appropriate and effective skills for managing the stress that remains.

Well-adjusted parents with thriving children tend to do this by controlling the two primary sources of stress in a child's life: the demands for performance and the demands for change. They control the demands for performance by keeping performance goals and expectations reasonable and achievable, with lots of free time where there are no performance expectations. They control the demands for change by limiting change in their child's life, particularly during times of inevitable and necessary upheaval like graduating from one school and entering another, or during a move.

They remain socially active. Thriving parents tend to be socially and emotionally active people. They remain active in church, school, and community events. They keep themselves emotionally invested in a cause or a purpose beyond their own as worthy of their time and energies.

Thriving Families Have Healthy Home Environments

Like adults, children don't thrive just anywhere. Some home environments are more conducive to healthy growth and development than others. It's not enough simply to plant a seed in the ground in order to raise a productive crop. The field must be tended, weeded, watered, and cared for during the early days and weeks of critical growth. Children, likewise, must be nurtured and provided an environment that aids their development rather than inhibiting it.

The home environment of thriving children tends to possess some or all of the following characteristics:

It's permanent. These families don't make frequent home changes. Again refer to Chapter 1 for a full discussion of this issue.

It's stable. The home environment, both physical and emotional climates, remains basically stable. Despite changing conditions outside the home and changing moods within individuals, a balance is maintained within the family for the welfare of all its members. Although these families acknowledge anger as an appropriate and healthy human response from time to time or in certain situations and the individual's right to become angry and express it, these families also acknowledge the right of all family members not to have the anger of one of its members capriciously inflicted upon them. Individual rights are respected, cooperation is encouraged, and special needs are met while preserving the health and unity of the family as a whole.

It's secure. The family is financially and socially secure. They aren't on the verge of financial or emotional bankruptcy. They have the resources necessary to meet the needs of individual family members as well as the family as a unit. The home is protected from intrusion and exploitation. It's truly a haven of peace and love for children as well as a laboratory for learning and development. It's well managed by the parents.

It's safe. The home is well constructed and maintained. Repairs are made quickly and effectively. There are no safety risks or hazards in the home for children. All dangerous chemicals are put away, out of reach of children. Cupboards and drawers are latched against the curious exploring of small children. There are adequate heating and cooling, ventilation, and space for the entire family. There are no exposed wires, uncovered electrical sockets, or unprotected open fires in the home. There are adequate toilet and bathing facilities within the home and a healthy level of sanitation and cleanliness is maintained. The children have play areas that are free of hazards and well protected.

It has routines. Family routines are important for children. They bring structure to their environment and make life predictable and manageable. Again, refer back to Chapter 1 for a full treatment of this important subject.

It has family traditions. Part of the glue that holds families together during hard times and supports family identity and togetherness is tradition. Members of a family are more likely to make the effort to get together for a holiday, for example, if it's traditional for them to do so. Common identities, beliefs, and purposes are shared in traditions. Practicing traditions within the family gives a child a strong sense of belonging as well as a sense of the continuity of life's events.

It celebrates life. Children thrive in environments that are positive and encouraging toward life and people. These families are opportunistic and optimistic, and they look for reasons to be happy and celebrate. Though they have their problems like all families, they seek out constructive, effective solutions to their problems. Every day is an adventure, always possessing an element of surprise.

It has clear values and beliefs. Ambiguity and uncertainty inhibit the healthy growth of children. Families in which children thrive tend to have a well ordered, clear value and belief system. There is a reason behind everything they do. They have a clear understanding of where they stand on most issues of concern to parents and families. Because of their clarity, these values and beliefs can be readily passed on to the children.

It has clear and appropriate roles. Thriving children have clear roles within the family. They have opportunities to share in the successful functioning of the family, particularly during high stress times. Having chores that are reasonable, appropriate for their age and capabilities, and not overly demanding teaches them to function within a system. It also instills responsibility, cooperation, and a sense of accomplishment. In addition to being allowed and encouraged to participate in family functions, thriving children tend to live in families where the generation lines are clear and distinct, where parents function in adult roles instead of always trying to be like their children. Parents who adopt the attitudes of their children or who attempt to dress like them, talk like them, or share the same tastes in music and other forms of art and recreation do their children a great disservice. Not only does it confuse the adult-child relationship, but it also doesn't give the children the opportunity to develop an identity apart from their parents. Also, thriving families don't experience role reversal, which occurs when the parent looks to the child for care and nurturing instead of being the provider.

It provides healthy models. Educators know that kids learn best through modeling—that is, copying the behavior of their parents, teachers, and other respected adults. Not only is this the most effective form of teaching, but it is also the most common form of learning for children. Children emulate those they want most to impress or are most eager to please. Thriving children live in families where the adults provide them strong, clear models. These children learn what it means to be male and female in a family, how best to resolve conflict and get what they want, what is important in life and what is not, and how to be self-disciplined—all from their parents.

Well-adjusted, happy families don't just happen. They are shaped by parents who care enough to learn and work at it.

Well-adjusted children and happy families, like most good things in life, don't just happen. They're made to happen! Such families are engineered by adults who know enough about what they're doing to care enough to try. These are people who don't blindly accept the ordinary as necessary but instead strive constantly for the extraordinary as possible. In seeking the good, they achieve the best.

Chapter 9
Helping Our Neighbors and Ourselves

"If I could tell you how to double your income this year, would you listen?" the man asked, his eyes probing deep into my own.

"Of course I would listen," I answered with a smile.

"If I could tell you how to trim one hundred dollars per month off your mortgage payment, would you want to hear that?" The question was addressed to me from across the room. I watched the man closely for some clue to what he was driving at.

"That would be nice," I answered.

"If I could tell you how to get ten more miles per gallon of gasoline in your car, would you want to know that, too?" the man continued, unrelenting. I was concentrating so hard on what the man was saying that I hardly noticed as he moved several steps closer to me.

"Yes," I answered.

"And what if I could tell you how to cut the cost of feeding your family in half. Would you listen to me?"

"Yes."

"You would?" he asked as he moved almost directly in front of me. "You would want me to tell you these things?"

"Well, of course!" I exclaimed. "I would be a fool not to want to know!"

"Yes, you would," he affirmed with a slight smile as he continued to watch me closely. "Now, if I could tell you how to possibly alter the course of world history, would you be interested?"

I was stunned. Alter the course of world history? Me? This strange man asking me strange questions had suddenly become even stranger.

"I don't know what you mean," I stated after a moment of hurriedly trying to collect my thoughts and make some sense of what he had asked. I was stalling for time.

"I mean that you have the power right there in your mind and in your heart and in your hands to do something so magnificent, so wonderful, and so incredibly powerful that you might well alter the course of world history! At the very least, I can promise that you will alter the course of history for at least one human being—perhaps many more!" The man paused for a moment to look long and hard at me. Surely he could see how confused I was by what he was saying. Could he also see that I was intrigued? "So, Phil, what do you say? Are you as interesting in altering world history as you are in saving money?"

"I don't know what you're talking about!" I snapped irritably. His questions were getting to me. For some reason I was feeling defensive. Maybe it was because all his questions were directed at me even though there were other people in the room. Maybe it was because he was now standing directly in front of me. Or maybe it was because of the tinge of guilt and self-consciousness I was beginning to feel as I suspected what was coming next.

"I'm talking about being a parent," he answered simply.

"Being a parent!" I exclaimed. Now I *was* irritated. "What does being a parent have to do with world history?"

"Lee Harvey Oswald altered world history," he responded without hesitation. "He had as much of an opportunity to grow up and become a president as to grow up and kill one!"

I was shocked. Even now as I remember this encounter with a teacher in junior college so long ago, I still feel some of the shock his statement sent racing through my mind. I had never thought of parenting as having long-term positive or negative consequences that could literally alter the course of world history. But as I listened to the man, I came to see that he was right. Children are born with incredible potentials: a potential for greatness or madness, for good or evil, for beauty or ugliness, for love or hate, for giving to the world the best of themselves or for taking from it what they need to survive. Which of the many potentials would become reality in any child would be determined largely by how he was raised.

But even as this awareness was dawning on me, my ego began to react to the implications of what the man had said. He was suggesting that I should be as interested in learning about being an effective parent as I was in doubling my income. This notion was troubling to me because I, like most people, believed I was already a good parent and had no need to learn how to become a better one. My kids were fed and clothed, and they had a home. Parenting, I believed then, is instinctual—it comes naturally to all those who have even an ounce of human blood flowing through their veins. It's a natural part of being human, not something to be learned in a classroom. There's no excuse for anyone's failing at it. Or so I thought.

I know now what that teacher was trying to tell me so long ago. Parenting is a tough job. It requires many skills, incredible understanding, great wisdom, patience, and commitment. But most of all, it requires compassion, the kind of compassion that leads us to care deeply and learn how to care effectively.

Learning to care effectively. What a simple statement that is but so full of meaning. It's not enough that we care. All parents care. But how many of us know how to care *effectively* about our children, to achieve the goals we have for them?

Most of us plunge into parenthood with no special training and with no support services available should the need arise. "Trust your instincts!" we're told. We do, and through a painful process of trial and error most of us are able to raise reasonably healthy children with a minimum of childhood scars. What a difference some preparation and training could have made! And what a difference some help along the way could have made also.

The man who confronted me with those hard questions in junior college was the teacher of a course entitled "The Sociology of the Family." He was suggesting to me that learning how to live should be of as much concern to me as learning how to make a living. Raising children and living together as a family are areas of serious concern in our society. After all, what value has a life well earned but poorly spent?

Preparing adequately for parenthood is an important part of being an effective and responsible parent. But just as important as that is knowing when to seek help once your children have arrived and you find yourself having trouble meeting their special needs.

When to Seek Help

Despite the pioneer spirit of self-sufficiency that still permeates our culture, all parents need help. Some of us need more than others. But all of us need the counsel, insight, techniques, and wisdom of others, particularly from those who have already raised their children. In earlier times, this help was usually available within the extended family where two, three, and perhaps even four generations lived together. But with the demise of the extended family, young parents find themselves alone with the awesome responsibility of having to raise and care for a totally dependent human being. They must do the best they can with what they have available. For many parents, this isn't enough. For all parents, this is less than it could be.

Knowing when to seek help is vital to effective parenting.

Knowing when to seek help is one of the most vital skills of effective parenting. It could well be the difference between success and failure. All families have problems. All problems have solutions. Finding the solution is the goal of effective parenting. Sometimes this means we must turn to outside help. The following guidelines will help you know when to seek outside help:

When you don't know what else to do. After you have tried everything you can think of to achieve an important goal with your child and all efforts have failed, get help. A baby who won't stop crying and a small child who persists in stealing from classmates at school, for example, are behaving as they do for a reason. The reason for their behavior must be dealt with before the behavior will change. For this, you will probably need help.

When you feel overwhelmed. Some situations are so painful and complex that they push us beyond our ability to cope normally. We feel overwhelmed and out of control. Marital or economic crises, for example, can make us feel disoriented, confused, and unsure of what to do or how to go about doing it. Trying to parent children during such times can be incredibly difficult. Get help.

When you feel trapped. Most of the time, life is an arena of vital activity for us. But occasionally it can become more like a prison. It can become boring, a real rut. We can begin to feel trapped by marriage, by economic responsibilities, by the demands of others, and by the kids. Feelings of entrapment tend to stir up other feelings that can inhibit effective parenting—for example, panic, great fear and anxiety, or perhaps just a powerful need to be free. Trapped people often become desperate people who will do almost anything to be set free. Such feelings could result in serious problems in the parent-child relationship. If you ever find yourself feeling this way, don't wait. Get help!

When you're afraid of what you might do. There are times in each of our lives when we're more emotionally volatile than others, when we're more likely to lash out at our kids, lose control of our tempers, do something we might later regret, or do something that might hurt ourselves or someone else. People who must live under a great deal of stress or in situations of serious deprivation for long periods of time are particularly vulnerable in this area. If you ever fear what you might do to your child, seek help immediately!

When you're hurting your child. Sometimes parents use techniques that they learned when they themselves were children but that do more harm than good. Sometimes parents can see the harmful effects these techniques are having on their children, but they continue to use them because they have been practiced in the family for so long. Remember, however, that being parented doesn't have to be a painful experience for children. It's possible to raise children without hurting them. If you're not sure about the techniques you're using, get help. Talk to someone about it, preferably a child development specialist.

When you're inhibiting your child. It's generally true that children grow up to be just like their parents. Some parents unwittingly pass on traits to their children that may inhibit their growth into healthy, well-adjusted adults. An overly submissive, dependent mother, for example, will likely raise her daughter to be overly submissive and dependent on males. Similarly, the painfully shy father typically does nothing to encourage his son to develop social skills. No teacher has a greater impact on the thinking and behavior of a child than a parent. If you're teaching your child ways of thinking and behaving that are more likely to set him up to fail than to succeed in life and relationships, get assistance. Learn how to help your child avoid your own mistakes.

When you think you need help. Most parents are pretty honest people. The greatest and most effective diagnostic tool we have to know when we need outside help is our own intuition, that "gut feeling" that something isn't quite right, that things aren't going as they should. Listen to your inner voice. If you suspect you need help with your child or with a particular problem, the chances are excellent that you do. Get it!

Recognizing those times when you need outside help is only the first step you need to take. It's meaningless to acknowledge the need and then do nothing about it. Helping yourself also involves action—doing something to get the needed help.

This is a real stumbling block for many parents who know they need help such as parental counseling or parenting classes. They believe, as I used to, that parenting is the one thing in all of life that you aren't supposed to be able to fail at doing. It comes naturally, the result of being human. Thus, they often fear the reactions of others who might find out they're seeking help. Their fear is of judgment, of people's thinking them somehow inadequate.

This is an irrational fear. All parents need help. Whether we acknowledge it or not, there isn't one of us who could not benefit from the wisdom and counsel of others. Only fools believe they're totally self-sufficient. The only parenting failures among us are those who refuse to seek help when they need it.

Helping Our Neighbors

It's one thing to help yourself. But how do you go about helping another parent who has a problem without hurting his feelings or offending him? There's a sense, after all, in which the health and welfare of every child is the rightful concern of all adults. Children's needs must be met by adults until they're old enough to take care of themselves—regardless of the source of the help. This is as true of children with parents as it is of those without them. We assume, of course, that children with parents will have their needs met by them. And in most cases, they do. But occasionally we come across parents who are saying or doing something to a child that is harmful. Is there a way to help these parents see what they're doing without angering or offending them?

This is one of the greatest concerns of people who care about children. It's easy to know what to do in a situation where another person is obviously hurt and in need of medical attention or when the offending person admits openly that he has a problem and needs help. But what's to be done for the parent who's unaware of the hurt he's causing, who doesn't know yet that a problem exists?

The health and welfare of every child is the rightful concern of all adults.

At the conclusion of one of my presentations, a woman approached me and asked if I could talk with her a moment. In the speech, I had called for adults everywhere to become as concerned about the welfare of all children as they are about the welfare of their own. Stating her desire to become a child advocate, the woman began telling me about her friend.

"Katy is one of the sweetest people I have ever met," she told me with obvious affection. "And she's a good mother. She takes really good care of her three children. But I'm concerned about her oldest daughter."

"Why are you concerned?" I asked.

"Well, she seems to expect more of her oldest than the rest. The child is only seven, and yet her mother treats her like she was ten or twelve, maybe. I know she doesn't mean to, but Katy is really hard on the girl sometimes. She yells a lot. And calls her names. And says mean things to her sometimes. She's so critical of the poor girl all the time. I know it must hurt her a lot. I can see it in her eyes, and the way she tries to hide sometimes. Is there any way I can help the child without hurting Katy? She's a special friend, and I don't want to lose her!"

Here are some suggestions I gave her at the time that you should follow also if you find yourself in a similar situation:

1. Confront the problem. Sit down with your friend and express your concerns in a caring, nonjudgmental manner. The object is to make the parent aware of what she's inadvertently doing to her child, not to make her feel guilty about it. This direct approach can be most helpful in strong, healthy rela-

tionships where you know the other person well, where there's some level of mutual trust and respect.

2. Empathize with the offender. During a visit over coffee or other opportunity, ask the following question: "Do you ever feel that one of your children lets you down on purpose? Like he's just doing it to hurt you or to get even?" Specify the particular behavior that is your concern. Using this question can open a door for the person to express some pent-up feelings of frustration that could be the cause of the problem. By empathizing with the offender, you're able to discuss the problem as two equally concerned parents. It also provides an opportunity to suggest solutions or other ways of dealing with it.

3. Ask for help. Sometimes it's easier for people to see themselves in the behavior of other people than to be confronted directly. Tell the person you have a problem and you need her help. Ask for her advice about how you might approach a good friend whom you don't want to offend but who is inadvertently hurting her child. Discuss the problem thoroughly. It won't take much for the offender to see herself in the situation and relate it directly to the way she's treating her own child.

4. Start a parents' group. All parents need the support of other parents who are experiencing similar kinds of things with their children. Invite a few of your friends, including the one you're concerned about, into your home for an informal get-together to discuss children and parenting. Then in the course of discussion, bring up the problem behavior that concerns you without identifying the parent involved. Approach it from an empathetic position rather than an accusatory one.

5. Model appropriate behavior. Whenever you're together with the parent and child about whom you're concerned, model alternative ways of dealing with the child. One of the best teaching techniques is showing how to do something. Many parents who hurt their children do so simply because they don't know any other way.

6. Set up some classes. Work to set up a parents' training program or parenting classes at school, through the PTA, or at

church. Then address the problem behavior in one of these sessions.

7. Suggest resources. Be prepared to suggest names of professionals a person can turn to for help if needed. Or have some books or articles available should you get a chance to recommend them.

8. Share new knowledge. Approach the person with a desire to share some new information you have learned from an article or a book you have just finished reading, from a lecture you attended, or from a program you watched on television. Sharing new insights can be one of the less threatening approaches to intervening on behalf of the child.

After discussing these options with the woman who came to me following my speech, I challenged her to choose one and make a sincere effort to help the child and her mother. She walked away a little more confident and with an assurance to me that she would do just that.

I was fortunate to meet the woman again. It was more than a year later, and I was back in her area of the country conducting another workshop. She came to me during lunch and reintroduced herself. I was eager to find out what had happened between her and her friend.

She told me she had spoken to Katy from the perspective of wanting to tell her what she had learned at an interesting workshop, and that gave her a chance to discuss with Katy some of the things parents can do that hurt their children emotionally and mentally. Katy had then admitted she was too hard on her daughter, and she has since worked hard to stop saying and doing the things that were the problem. Now the two women get together with a couple of other mutual friends on a regular basis to talk about parenting.

There were tears in the woman's eyes as she gave me a hug right there in the middle of a busy restaurant. "You want to know something funny, Phil?" she asked. "Being in that group has helped me be a better parent as much as it has Katy!"

Chapter 10
Honey Bunch

The other day I was irritated and frustrated while trying to accomplish a task that should have been easy but that I had somehow made agonizingly difficult. In the midst of my simmering, my two-year-old daughter approached with a book held at arm's length toward me.

"You read to Morgan, please?" her sweet voice asked without fear.

"No! No, go away! Papa's busy!" I barked at her. I didn't mean to shout at her, but all the frustration of the moment focused on her intrusion into my consciousness at that moment.

At first I saw questioning in her eyes as though she didn't comprehend my answer. But it was soon replaced by a look of hurt. As she lowered her eyes and began to turn away, I became suddenly aware that she and I would never again have that particular moment together. It would come only once in our lifetime. Now I, as an adult, had a choice of whether to take that moment and make it into something really special for both of us, or let it slip away. It was then that I also remembered Morgan was a gift from God, a child placed into my care for a few short years to raise as one of His own. She wouldn't always be there with me. The day would come when she would leave.

Focusing now on the opportunity that moment offered me, I

reached out and took her into my lap. Hugging her close, I apologized for snapping at her.

"Papa's sorry he yelled at you, Sweetheart. Of course I'll read you a story!"

With eyes still brimming with tears but now accompanied by a light as bright as the smile on her face, she accepted my apology.

"It's okay, Honey Bunch!" she squealed.

Never before had I known such a depth of love as I did at that moment. The love of that child for me was so unquestioning, her trust so complete, and her forgiveness so ready. How could my love and respect for her be anything less?

It was then I decided that I would treat my two-year-old daughter as I would any other human life not a part of my family. I would give her the same respect I would give you or your children. I would not do or say to her what I would not do or say to you.

As I basked in the joy of that very special moment with my daughter, I knew without doubt that Dorothy Law Nolte was right when she wrote the following poem.

Children Learn What They Live*

If a child lives with criticism, he learns to condemn.
If a child lives with hostility, he learns to fight.
If a child lives with ridicule, he learns to be shy.
If a child lives with shame, he learns to feel guilty.
If a child lives with tolerance, he learns to be patient.
If a child lives with encouragement, he learns confidence.
If a child lives with praise, he learns to appreciate.
If a child lives with fairness, he learns justice.
If a child lives with security, he learns to have faith.
If a child lives with approval, he learns to like himself.
If a child lives with acceptance and friendship, he learns to
    find love in the world.

This is the well-adjusted child.

*Used by special permission of Dorothy Law Nolte, Ph.D., 1972.

Bibliography

For Additional Reading

Ames, Louise Bates and Frances L. Ilg. *Your Two Year Old: Terrible or Tender*. New York: Dell, 1976.

Balter, Lawrence and Anita Shreve. *Dr. Balter's Child Sense*. New York: Poseidon Publishers, 1985.

Briggs, Dorothy C. *Your Child's Self-esteem*. New York: Dolphin Books, 1975.

Campbell, Ross. *How to Really Love Your Child*. Wheaton: Victor Books, 1977.

Durkin, Lisa L. *Parents and Kids Together*. New York: Warner Books, 1986.

Elkind, David. *The Hurried Child*. Massachusetts: Addison-Wesley Publishing Company, 1981.

Frailberg, Selma H. *The Magic Years*. New York: Charles Scribner's Sons, 1959.

Ginott, Haim G. *Between Parent and Child*. New York: McGraw-Hill, 1961.

Maglish, Elaine and Adele Faber. *How to Talk So Kids Will Listen and Listen So Kids Will Talk*. New York: Avon, 1980.

Riddell, Carole and Kay Wallingford. *Helpful Hints for Fun-Filled Parenting*. Nashville: Thomas Nelson, 1984.

Rogers, Fred and Barry Head. *Mister Rogers Talks with Parents*. New York: Berkley Books, 1983.

Rosenberg, Ellen. *Growing Up Feeling Good*. New York: Beaufort Books, 1983.

ICARE

ICARE (International Child Advocacy and Resource Enterprises) was founded by Phil Quinn in June 1983 as a means of providing public and professional education in the areas of child abuse, neglect, emotional assault and deprivation, and child sexual abuse. It is a nonprofit organization whose goal is primary prevention—that is, preventing child abuse before it occurs, before there is tragedy.

Since its founding, ICARE has grown into a volunteer movement of hundreds of caring persons all across the country. To date it has sponsored more than two hundred professional training programs and an equal number of public awareness projects. It is involved in counseling programs for victims and perpetrators and is planning several innovative primary prevention projects.

If you would like to know more about the work of ICARE or how you might become a member and get involved, write to Dr. Quinn at the following address:

ICARE
P.O. Box 499
Hermitage, Tennessee 37076-0499